CURRENT ADVANCES IN COMMUNITY SCIENCE

(Peer Reviewed Book)

CURRENT ADVANCES IN COMMUNITY SCIENCE

Dr. Khushboo Gupta, Assistant Professor, Trilok Singh TT College, Lakshmangarh, Sikar, Rajasthan, India

Dr. Deepa Swamy, Professor and Head, Dept. of Home Science, Govt. Arts Girls College, Kota, Rajasthan, India

Prof. Sadhna Jain, Professor, Dept. of Human Development and Family Empowerment, Aditi Mahavidyalaya, University of Delhi, Delhi, India

Dr. Sangeeta, Professor, Home- Science (Food & Nutrition), Ramabai Govt. Women Post Graduate College- Akbarpur, Ambedkar Nagar- Uttar- Pradesh,

Dr. Chetna Rochani, MD (Hom), PG-FHPC, Associate Professor & amp; HOD, Department of Pathology, P P Savani University, Kosamba, Surat.

Dr. Richa Verma, Assistant Professor, Department of Home Science, Dayalbagh Educational Institute, Dayalbagh, Agra, India

NOTION PRESS

NOTION PRESS

India. Singapore. Malaysia.

Published by Notion Press
Publication Year 2023

ISBN: 9798891860872

Amount: Rs. 499/- (In India)

US $ 16.99 (Outside India)

CONTENTS

PREFACE

The edited book volume is primarily intended to be a collection of peer reviewed and plagiarism free chapters written by research scholars, academicians, scientists, doctors and faculty members of their respective fields. Chapters of this book entitled "Current Advances in Community Science" particularly based on topics such as impact and benefits of nano-fertilizers, understanding the benefits of dietary fibres on health, importance of food fortification, consumer problems and protection in India related to adulteration, black marketing, health and psychological well-being, role of millets to sustain food and nutritional security, extension education in modern era, paradigm shift in extension approaches for sustainable development, computer aided designing in textiles and apparel industry, use of microfibers, Instagram as a tool to promote micro apparels and qualitative analysis on the different areas of skill development in community science.

We envisage this book to serve as a professional reference for researchers and practitioners in their relevant scientific field. This book will be very useful for students all over in India and Abroad, academicians, public health specialists, community science specialists, community development professionals, programmers of national and international agencies, entrepreneurs and aspirants of new start ups/ enterprises as well as libraries of relevant collages and institutions.

This book should be of interest to policy makers, bureaucrats, economists and community scientists and can be a reference material development industry.

This is the Twelfth book in the series of community upliftment. You can see the details of previous books in the section of list of publication at the end of the book.

With great pleasure, we would like to extend our sincere thanks to all the authors of the chapters for reporting their thoughts and experience related to their research and also for patiently addressing reviewer's comments and diligently adhering hectic deadlines to have the book published in timely manner. Their constant support and cooperation has made our task as editors a pleasure. We believe that this book is an important contribution to the community in addressing research work from numerous domains of community science and community development.

It is our sincere hope that many more will join us in this time-critical endeavour and this book will stimulate discussions and generate helpful comments to improve future projects.

Happy reading and feedback awaited.

Dr. Khushboo Gupta
Dr. Deepa Swamy
Prof. Sadhna Jain
Dr. Sangeeta
Dr. Chetna Rochani
Dr. Richa Verma

INTRODUCTION

Dr. Khushboo Gupta

Assistant Professor

Trilok Singh TT College

Lakshmangarh, Sikar (Rajasthan)

Email: drkhushboogupta2017@gmail.com

Community Science is an interdisciplinary field of study having a scientific understanding of the community concerned and to improve the quality of life of individuals, family and people at large. Previously this discipline is known as home science but it was changed as community science as there has been a nation wise change of nomenclature as per 5th dean's committee recommendations to widen the scope for employability of the graduates/ postgraduates.

In this discipline a student learn basic fundamental things to advanced knowledge regarding different subjects i.e. food science and nutrition, human development, clothing and textile, home management, family studies, family resource management and consumer science, extension education and communication management etc. The knowledge needs to be revised to keep pace with the advancement in technology and changing needs of the society.

Community science is a conceptual domain dedicated to societal development through proper science and technological tools. Community science may be bring as both, individual course of study or may be an individual subject. It is an interdisciplinary subject. Interdisciplinary means connection between some subjects irrespective of domain and direct and indirect connection with main facet or sub fields.

Community is actually a social unit of any size that shares common values; however the embodied or face to face community is usually treated as small, large or more extended communities.

Science is refers to this body of knowledge itself, of the type that can be rationally explained and reliably applied. Knowledge of community science is very essential because our world faces critical challenges that are multidisciplinary in nature and exist at the intersection of science and society; climate change, public health preparedness, systemic disparities in health outcomes and the opportunities and risks associated with rapidly developing technologies such as artificial intelligence, automation and robotics.

Advancement in community science often involves using scientific methods, processes and tools to collect data and observations, that also incorporate data analysis to envision the actual situation. This helps to understand the current circumstances and priorities of community including applying this knowledge to cater their needs and make them self sufficient, independent, self reliable and economically sustainable.

In India G20 summit was organized in New Delhi on 9th and 10th September 2023 with the theme of **"Vasudhaiva Kutumbakam"** which means **"One earth, One family,**

One future". In this global summit, supreme leaders of 20 nations talked about different issues. Among them, sustainable development goal is one of the prime issues that need acceleration in progress. Leaders commit to taking collection action for effective and timely implementation of the G20 2023 action plan to accelerate progress on the sustainable development goals.

In year 2015, the united nation adopted 17 sustainable development goals as a universal call to action to end poverty, to protect the planet and to ensure that by year 2030 all people enjoy peace and prosperity. These goals are integrated - it means action in one area affects in outcomes of other area, thus the development must have balance in social, economical and environment sustainability.

In this global summit leaders said that they will ensure that no more is left behind and everyone can get proper food, livelihood, basic health facilities, proper nutrition and energy that are necessary to improve quality of life of the community personals.

Implementation of the advance knowledge of community science provided in this book **"Current Advances in Community Science"** can be worked as a milestone in this direction.

Happy reading and feedback awaited.

BIOGRAPHY
(DR. KHUSHBOO GUPTA)

Dr. Khushboo Gupta is a PhD Home Science (Food Science and Nutrition) from Banasthali Vidyapith, Newai, India. She has been teaching subject including food chemistry, food analysis, therapeutic nutrition, human nutrition, human physiology and community nutrition, etc. Presently she is working as Assistant Professor in Trilok Singh TT College, Laxmangarh, Sikar, Rajasthan.

She is MSc Gold medalist and had **cleared UGC-NET and RPSC-SET examination.** Dr Gupta holds Advance Diploma in French Language from Banasthali Vidyapith; Diploma in Naturopathy and Yoga (NDDY) from Gandhi Smarak Prakritik Chikitsa Samiti (Regd.), New Delhi; Certificate in Homeopathic Medicinal System conducted by Vardhman Mahaveer Open University, Kota and Certificate in Statistical Techniques and Applications. She has featured in several programs of All India Radio and Radio Banasthali (FM 90.4).

Dr. Khushboo is actively involved in community activities especially those concerned with self-employment, health and wellness, optimum nutrition and how to improve quality of life of a person and family. She is the keynote speaker and founder of her YouTube channel "Dietitian Ki Salah" through which she provides education related to optimum health, wellness and nutrition to masses. Dr. Gupta has published about more than 30 research papers in reputed national and international journals; 5 book chapters in five different edited books, several news paper and magazine articles related to health, nutrition and new food product formulation. She authored one book related to elderly nutrition; edited eleven books related to community science, food science and nutrition, health and wellness, issues with girls and millets for upliftment of the individuals of the society. She presented her research work in more than 25 national and international conferences. Her research is primarily in the area of food processing entrepreneurial skill Inculcation and geriatric nutrition. **The patent office, Government of India has granted a patent to Dr. Khushboo for her research on food formulation using RSM.** Dr. Gupta has successfully completed more than 30 courses on various diverse topics organized by SWAYAM, UNICEF, WHO and Cornell University.

In past she had worked as Assistant Professor (Food and Nutrition) in Modi University, Laxmangarh, Sikar; worked as Master Trainer in Agriculture University, Kota. During her PhD she had worked as UGC- SRF in Banasthali Vidyapith, Newai. One feather in her cap is that she had worked as regular trainee dietitian in dietetics department of Post Graduate Institute of Medical Education and Research (PGIMER), Chandigarh and got her short-term attachment certificate. She won many awards in different seminars and conferences for her contribution in scientific world. Apart from them, she is rewarded with Teacher Honour award by Lions Club Kota South (September, 2017) and 'Award of Honour' given by All Rajasthan Qualified Homoeopathic Doctors Association in Homoeopathic Scientific Seminar, 2017.

She is the life member of many reputed institutes i.e. Nutrition Society of India, Indian Dietetic Association, The Indian Science Congress Association and Institute of Scholars and giving her services for upliftment of community.

BIOGRAPHY
(DR. DEEPA SWAMY)

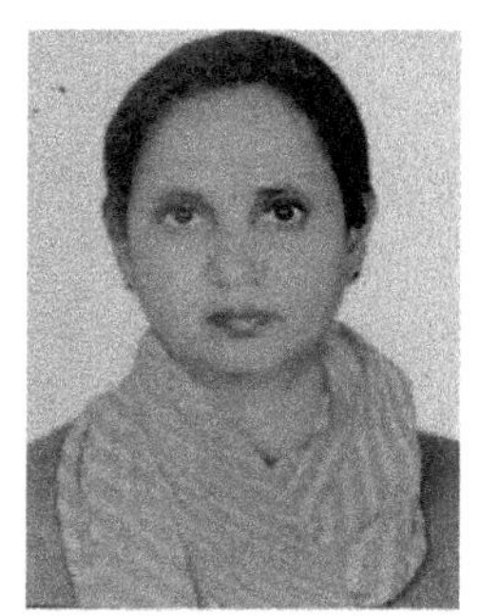

Dr. Deepa Swamy is presently working as Professor and head in Dept. of Home science; Government Arts Girls College, Kota (Rajasthan). She has completed her graduation (1997) and post graduation (1999) from Maharana Pratap Agriculture University, Udaipur. She is convener of BOS (Home Science), member of academic council and examiner selection committee in Home Science at University of Kota, Kota (Rajasthan) from last 2 years. She is also an approved IGNOU counselor for the course of NHE and CFN. Also serving as an academic counselor at Vardhman Mahaveer Open University, kota from the last 5 years. She has more than 21 years of teaching and research experience. She is life member of many reputed community and society. Dr. Swamy has published many research papers in national and international journals. Four book chapters in different edited books, several magazines articles and three reference books are her major publications.

Apart from that she is also awarded by Government of Rajasthan for her teaching work.

BIOGRAPHY (PROF. SADHNA JAIN)

Prof Sadhna Jain has over two decades of teaching experience in the Department of Human Development and Family Empowerment at Aditi Mahavidyalaya, University of Delhi, Delhi. She has done M.Sc., B. Ed, M.Ed., M.Phil., and a Ph.D. She received a gold medal for her doctoral work. She has qualified National Eligibility Test twice and the Delhi Subordinate Services Recruitment Board competitive exam. She has actively participated in the curriculum design of various courses of different levels, and administrative roles, and has attended numerous workshops and Faculty Development Programmes. Her publications include papers in national/international journals of repute and book chapters. She has completed research projects funded by UGC, the research council, etc., provided research guidance to undergraduate students, and worked philanthropically as a consultant for an NGO working in the field of HIV/AIDS. Additionally, she has organized conferences, workshops, webinars, FDPs, etc. She also supervises dissertations of the M.Sc. Counselling and Family Therapy course run by Indira Gandhi National Open University, Delhi. She plans to continue contributing to holistic teaching, research, and professional development.

BIOGRAPHY
(DR. SANGEETA)

Dr. Sangeeta is working as Assistant Professor in Home- Science (Food & Nutrition) at Ramabai Govt. Women Post Graduate College- Akbarpur, Ambedkarnagar- Uttar- Pradesh. She has 13 year experience of teaching to graduates and Post graduate students. She Qualifies the U. G. C. NET Examination in June 2005. Her more than 30 research papers have been published in National and International Journals and Proceedings of seminars as well as 10 Book chapters published from National and International Publishers. She has more than 10 societies and institutional life Membership

She got many prestigious awards such as Best Teacher Award, Young Scientist Award; Award from Higher Education, Excellence Academician Award, Best Oral Presentation Award etc. she had organized 6 webinars and 05 International Conferences. She wrote a book and edited 2 books.

BIOGRAPHY
(DR. CHETNA ROCHANI)

Dr. Chetna Rochani, is a passionate Homoeopath and a dedicated teacher, from Vadodara, Gujarat, India. She studied B.H.M.S from Baroda Homeopathic Medical and MD Homoeopathy (Materia Media) from R.K. Anand Homeopathic College and Research Institute. She also received an N.D.D.Y. (Diploma in Naturopathy and Diploma in Yoga) from Gandhi National Academy of Naturopathy. She also completed PG-FHPC-Fellowship Course in Homoeopathic Psychiatry &Counseling, from MUHS, Nashik. She is always ready to accept the challenging cases with deeper pathological conditions, psychiatric cases, surgical cases as well most challenging cases of **Autistic children**.

She has received awards from Bhartiya Sindhu Sabha, Warshiya Sindhi Sewa Samite, Harni Gurudwara Committee, Warashiya Gurudwara Committee for rendering excellent service in Homeopathy. Also conducting free monthly camps on thyroid and diabetes and health awareness programs. Also received Diamond Homoeo Award by Kiran Seva Sansthan, MP, Rewa. She follows the philosophy: "Everything is possible in Homoeopathy only if you choose to remain a hardworking and dedicated student throughout the life".

BIOGRAPHY
(DR. RICHA VERMA)

Dr. Richa Verma is working as Assistant Professor in Department of Home Science, Dayalbagh Educational Institute, Dayalbagh, Agra, India since March 2010. She has teaching and research guiding experience of 14 years; Awarded Director Medal for M.Sc. (Home Science). Her main area of research is early childhood care and education, adolescent development, and family studies in the light of Human behavior; Human personality; Family and community sciences; Developmental aspects of humans; Children with special needs; Family dynamics. Guiding 24 M.Sc. /M.Phil. Dissertations and PhD, Three PhD Candidate awarded and supervising four Ph.D. candidates.

She received 04 best research paper/national awards. She has 25 research papers and 04 chapters in edited books. She is in editorial board of 03 reputed international journals and is member of 5 professional societies and served as scientific committee member in 6 national/international conferences. Apart from this, she has participated in approx. 30 national/ international conferences and training programs and delivered 10 talks and guest lectures in workshops/training programs and organized 02 workshops/training programs. Successfully Completed over 100 Webinars, Workshops, Courses, training programs organized by prestigious institutions as UGC, AICTE, IITs, NITs, UNICEF, Coursera, Udemy, etc.

LIST OF CONTRIBUTORS

1. **Anita Raj**, Lecturer, Govt. PG. College, Panchkula, Chandigarh
2. **Bhavna**, Department of Foods and Nutrition, CCS HAU, Hisar, Haryana- 125004
3. **Dr. Achal Shetty**, Assistant Professor, Community Medicine Father Muller Medical College, Mangalore, Karnataka-575002
4. **Dr. Alka Pandey** Assistant Professor, Department of Psychology, School of Liberal Education, Galgotias University, Uttar Pradesh
5. **Dr. Ashakiran Srinivasaiah**, , Assistant Professor, Biochemistry Haveri Institute of Medical Sciences, Haveri, Karnataka-581110
6. **Dr. Beenu Singh**, G. B. Pant University of Agriculture and Technology, Pantnagar Uttarakhand
7. **Dr. Bindu Chaturvedi,** Head of Department of Garment Production and Export Management Government Arts Girls College, Kota
8. **Dr. Garima Pathak**, Department of Botany, B.D.College, Patliputra University, Patna, India-800001
9. **Dr. Harish Rangareddy**, Assistant Professor, Biochemistry Haveri Institute of Medical Sciences, Haveri, Karnataka-581110

10. **Dr. Preeti verma,** Subject Matter Specialist (Home Science), Krishi Vigyan Kendra, Banasthali Vidyapith,

11. **Dr. Shalini Kumari,** Assistant Professor, Department of Psychology, School of Liberal Education, Galgotias University, Uttar Pradesh

12. **Dr.Lakshmi.S**, Assistant Professor, BNVCTE Thiruvallam, Thiruvananthapuram Kerala

13. **Manisha Gahlot,** G. B. Pant University of Agriculture and Technology, Pantnagar Uttarakhand

14. **Mrs. Anitha Misquith**, Assistant Professor, Biochemistry Sapthagiri Institute of Medical Sciences & Research Center, Bengaluru, Karnataka-560090

15. **Naresh Kumar**, Subject Matter Specialist (Horticulture), Krishi Vigyan Kendra, Banasthali Vidyapith,

16. **Neha**, Department of Foods and Nutrition, CCS HAU, Hisar, Haryana- 125004

17. **Nikita Sachwani**, Research Scholar , Department of Garment Production and Export Management Govt. Arts Girls College, Kota, University of Kota, Kota

18. **Pooja Gaba**, Creative Head, Craftales, New Delhi

19. **Raman Bharti**, PhD Scholar, Department of Extension Education and Communication Management, CCAS, MPUAT, Udaipur, Rajasthan

20. **Raveena**, Department of Foods and Nutrition, CCS HAU, Hisar, Haryana- 125004

21. **Rupanagudi Beena Fareq**, PhD Scholar, Apparel and Textile Sciences, College of Community Science,University of Agricultural Sciences, Dharwad, Karnataka

22. **Rupanagudi Unesha Fareq**, PhD Scholar, Family Resource Management, College of Home Science, GB Pant University of Agriculture and Technology, Pantnagar, Uttarakhand

23. **Seema Chawla,** Assistant Professor, Krishi Vigyan Kendra Sriganganagar, (Swami Keshwanand Rajasthan Agricultural University), Rajasthan

24. **Sonia**, Department of Foods and Nutrition, CCS HAU, Hisar, Haryana- 125004

If readers have any query related to any chapter of the book, kindly contact with the corresponding author of the chapter. Authors of the chapters are responsible for their work.

1.

THE IMPACT AND BENEFITS OF NANO-FERTILISER ON AGRICULTURE: A REVOLUTIONARY APPROACH

Dr. Garima Pathak

Department of Botany, B.D.College, Patliputra University, Patna, India-800001

Email: Garimapathak1309@gmail.com

Abstract

Nanotechnology has made incredible strides in a variety of industries recently, including agriculture. In significant part, nitrogen fertilization contributes to maintaining soil fertility and improving crop output and quality. Horticulture crops need precise nutrient management since they depend on chemical fertilizers, which is a big issue on a worldwide scale. Traditional fertilizers not only cost the producer a lot of money, but they may also be harmful to the environment and humans. This has led to the search for fertilizers that are acceptable from an ecological standpoint, particularly those with great nutrient-use efficiency. Nanotechnology is emerging as a potential replacement. Nanofertilizers are advantageous in managing nutrition because of their substantial potential to increase nutrient consumption efficiency. Nutrients are bound to nano-dimensional adsorbents, whether used alone or in combination, causing them to release nutrients much more slowly than they would with conventional fertilizers. The use of nanofertilizers in agriculture is examined in this article, along with the potential advantages, drawbacks, and implications of doing so. With this approach, less fertilizer is lost to groundwater while also increasing the effectiveness of nutrient use. Additionally, nanofertilizers may be used to boost a plant's ability to withstand abiotic stress. When mixed with microorganisms, these so-called nanobiofertilizers provide a number of additional benefits. Even though nanofertilizers have undoubtedly created new opportunities for sustainable agriculture, their disadvantages must also be carefully considered before being put on the market. Nanoparticles released into the environment or the food chain at large may be harmful to humans. As a result, not all nanomaterials will be equally safe for all applications, even though using nanofertilizers in agriculture has tremendous potential to improve plant nutrition and stress tolerance to create higher yields in a climate of climate change.

Keywords: Nanofertiliser, Agriculture, crop productivity, sustainable agriculture, microfertiliser, Nanobiofertiliser

1. Introduction

The United Nations has set 17 sustainable development objectives, one of which is "Zero Hunger," and sustainable agriculture is essential to achieving this goal. Due to rising water and energy costs as well as increased demands for water and energy, global food production and distribution are under tremendous strain. The quantity of resources used by modern agriculture is staggering. The three billion metric tons of crops grown annually around the world require 187 million metric tons of fertilizer, 4 million metric tons of pesticides, 2.7 trillion cubic meters of water (roughly 70% of all freshwater consumed globally), and more than two quadrillion British thermal units (BTU) of energy (Kah *et al.*, 2019). This situation necessitates massive changes to the world's food production systems. In order to promote food production and security, recent studies have revealed the promising potential of nanotechnology to improve the agricultural sector by increasing the efficiency of agricultural inputs and providing answers to challenges associated to agriculture and the environment. As a result, there has lately been a lot of interest in research on using nanotechnology in agriculture (Parisi *et al.*, 2015; Kah *et al.*, 2019). Chemical fertilizers provide the nutrients that plants require for their best development and production, yet current agricultural practices cannot fulfill the expanding food demand without using fertilizers extensively. The restricted nutrient utilization efficiency and environmental constraints associated with the use of chemical fertilizers continue to be a major problem and impediment to achieving respectable sustainability in agriculture.

The cost increases brought on by the overuse of chemical fertilizers also lower producers' profit margins. High conventional fertilizer release rates that exceed plant nutrient absorption rates and/or fertilizers or nutrients being transformed into forms that are not bioavailable to crops are common causes of low nutrient utilization efficiency (Chhipa, 2017). Because of this, there is a lot of interest in creating new fertilizer sources that can increase fertilizer effectiveness (Van Eerd *et al.*, 2017). A few techniques that have been proposed to increase fertilizer consumption efficiency include the use of precision fertilization, division or targeted application, fertigation, and the use of nanofertilizers (Lu *et al.*, 2018).

Applying nanotechnology to the development of new types of fertilizers is one of the most promising ways to significantly increase global horticultural production in order to meet the expanding food demands of the population while also being sustainable in the face of climate change (Raliya *et al.*, 2017; Feregrino-Perez *et al.*, 2018). Nanofertilizers have the ability to feed plants gradually and under controlled circumstances when used correctly (Chhipa and Joshi, 2016), while also increasing the effectiveness of fertilizer use, lowering leaching and volatilization, and lowering environmental concerns (Solanki *et al.*, 2016). According to the research discussed above, certain nanofertilizers can increase crop yields by enhancing plant stress tolerance, germination rates, seedling development, photosynthesis, nitrogen metabolism, and protein and carbohydrate synthesis. Nanofertilizers provide a number of advantages, including the ability to be administered with significantly less, which saves transportation costs and facilitates application. The business potential of nanofertilizers may be constrained by a few disadvantages.

2. What are nanofertilisers?

The past fifty years have seen a significant increase in agricultural yield, especially for grains, which has allowed for the majority of the world's nutritional demands to be satisfied. The growing use of chemical fertilizers is one of the primary reasons for increasing crop yield in this regard. The use of chemical fertilizers has expanded due to the variety of crops that benefit from fertilizer. Chemical fertilizers have a low utilization efficiency, which restricts their use since they lose fertilizer through leaching and volatilization, which harms the environment and drives up production costs (FAO, 2017). According to DeRosa (2010), typical fertilizers, for instance, lose between 50 and 70 percent of the nitrogen they add to the soil. The scientific community is thus closely monitoring the creation of substitute techniques to guarantee the sustainable use of nutrients. In this context, the use of nanotechnology enables the creation of slow-release fertilizers, the decrease of mobile nutrient losses, and the improvement of nutrient accessibility (Kah *et al.*, 2018). According to Kah *et al.* (2018), nanomaterials are either nutrients themselves (micro or macro nutrients) or act as nutrients themselves (transporters or additives for the nutrients, such as by composing with minerals). Nanomaterials can also be used to create nanofertilizers by enclosing nutrients inside them (DeRosa, 2010).

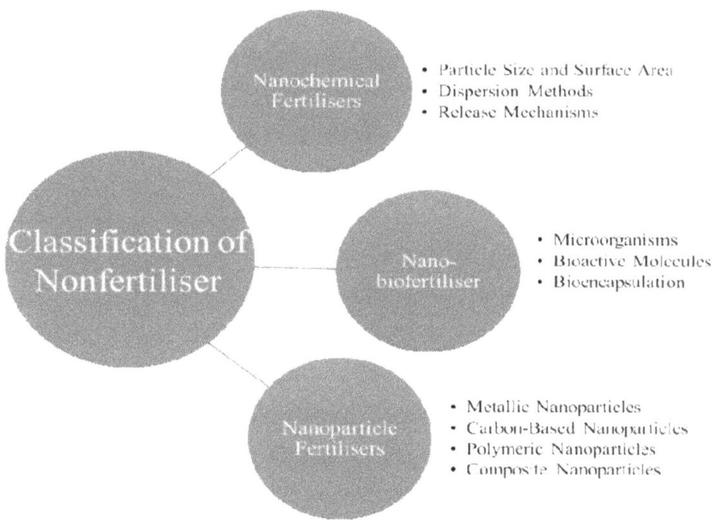

Figure 1: A taxonomy of nanofertilizers

3. Advantage of nanofertilisers

In order to fulfill the continually rising demands of the continuously growing human population, the agricultural sector is under increasing pressure. According to Ferregrino-Perez *et al.* (2018), synthetic fertilizers are widely employed in a variety of ways and are considered crucial for enhancing crop productivity. Although crops normally only absorb approximately half of the fertilizer applied (Chen and Wei, 2018), the remaining minerals may leach into the soil and contaminate nearby bodies of water (Liu and Lal, 2015). For instance, it has been demonstrated that the major macronutrients N, P, and K that are applied to the soil are lost at rates of 40–70%, 80–90%, and 50–90%, respectively (Feregrino-Perez *et al.*, 2018; Solanki *et al.*, 2016; Chen and Wei, 2018). Gardeners often apply these fertilizers repeatedly in order to achieve the desired yields. However, this method has the potential to lower soil fertility and increase salt concentrations, which might lead to crop losses in the future. Additionally, unregulated nutrient delivery has the potential to result in uneven fertilization and worse crop quality. In order to increase crop output and quality, as well as sustainability in horticultural production, slow-release fertilizers must be created (Feregrino-Perez *et al.*, 2018). The use of non-chemical fertilizers is presently in intense demand in the horticulture sector in order to considerably increase food security (Chen and Wei, 2018). Innovative strategies and cutting-edge technology are necessary for the horticulture sector to experience sustainable economic and environmental growth. Nanomaterials are often defined as having a size of 100 nm or less in at least one dimension (Kah, 2015; Kim *et al.*, 2018). These materials serve as the building blocks of nanotechnology (Monreal *et al.*, 2016).

Nanomaterials include single- or multiwalled nanotubes, magnetic iron nanoparticles, copper, aluminum, silver, gold, zinc, zinc oxide, silica, cerium oxide, titanium dioxide, and tin oxide. Tan *et al.* (2017); Raliya *et al.* (2015); 2016; Raliya *et al.* (2015) Nanoparticles can be employed effectively in the development and usage of novel fertilizers because they have special qualities such as a high surface-to-volume ratio, controlled-release kinetics to specific regions, and sorption capacity (Feregrino-Perez *et al.*, 2018). According to Zuverza-Mena *et al.* (2017), nanofertilizers are nutrients that have been encapsulated or coated with nanomaterials to control and feed one or more nutrients slowly in order to satisfy the basic dietary requirements of plants. These "smart fertilizers" are currently thought to be a promising option (Rameshaiah *et al.*, 2015), often to the point that they are preferred to conventional fertilizers (Iavicoli *et al.*, 2017; Dimkpa *et al.*, 2017). Due to fertilizers' contact with plants and the high reactivity of nanomaterials, plants absorb nutrients and significant chemicals more effectively and efficiently (Prasad *et al.*, 2017). Nanofertilizer absorption, dispersion, and accumulation in crops will be highly impacted by both intrinsic and extrinsic characteristics, as well as the route of exposure, which all depend on the efficiency of nanofertilizers. The two internal characteristics that have the most impact on how effectively nanoparticles function are particle size and surface coatings. Other significant environmental parameters that impact how well nanoparticles may be employed include organic matter, soil texture, and pH (El-Ramady *et al.*, 2018; Ma *et al.*, 2018). Additionally, the exposure route and manner of delivery have a significant impact on the behavior, bioavailability, and absorption of nanofertilizers by crops (El-Ramady *et al.*,

2018). Utilizing nanofertilizers in agriculture might increase the likelihood that global food production will be sustainable. There is a huge burden on the food production industry since the use of less nutrient-dense foods and a poor dietary intake of fruits and vegetables are the main causes of nutritional inadequacies in human populations (Cornelis *et al.*, 2014).

Nanofertilizers provide a number of benefits over conventional chemical fertilizers, including their method of nutrient delivery (Liu and Lal, 2015). Through slow or controlled release methods, they manage how readily available nutrients are to crops. The coating or cementing of nutrients with nanoparticles has been linked to slow nutrition delivery (Solanki *et al.*, 2016). This technique of progressive nutrient delivery, which provides plants with nutrients constantly over a lengthy period of time, may enable farmers to boost crop development. For instance, nitrogen delivery can be delayed from the typical 4–10 days observed in traditional fertilizers to 40–50 days (Chen and Wei, 2018). When fertilizer is applied using traditional techniques, half of it either leaches away or is too much for the plant to consume. This may have either positive or negative effects on the plant. Through slow or controlled release methods, they manage how readily available nutrients are to crops. According to Solanki *et al.* (2016), nutrient delivery delays have been linked to nanoparticle coating or cementing. Application and shipping expenses can be cut with nanofertilizers, according to research (Fan, 2014). The soil is not weighted down by salts, which are often prone to being treated excessively when using traditional fertilizers over the course of a short- or long-term period, as a result of applying modest amounts (León-Silva *et al.*, 2018). The precise nutritional needs of the crops that will be cultivated may be catered for using nanofertilizers (Kah *et al.*, 2018). Biosensors can be connected to a new, special fertilizer in this regard to regulate the delivery of nutrients based on the state of the soil's nutrients, the stage of crop growth, or environmental circumstances (León-Silva *et al.*, 2018). Plants are sensitive to the availability of micronutrients during crop growth; as a result, fruits and vegetables with low nutritional value are produced (López-Valdez *et al.*, 2018; Srivastava and Malhotra, 2017). Nanofertilizers, however, allow farmers the opportunity to apply adequate quantities of nutrients (Feregrino-Perez *et al.*, 2018; Kyriacou and Rouphael, 2018). Micronutrient distribution to a specific crop may be very difficult to regulate using a regular nutrient management system. For instance, the majority of horticulture-producing regions worldwide are deficient in certain micronutrients, such as Zn and Fe (López-Valdez *et al.*, 2018). As a result, nanofertilizers are a suitable fortification method for crops and fresh foods. The bioavailability of nutrients is increased by nanofertilizers due to their high specific surface area, tiny size, and high reactivity (Liu and Lal, 2015). On the other hand, the plant can resist a variety of biotic and abiotic problems when it receives appropriate nourishment from nanofertilizers, which has clear overall advantages. However, the widespread use of nanofertilizers in agriculture may have some serious downsides, which have been discussed in more depth below (Figure 2).

4. Crop response to nanofertilizers

By more efficiently utilizing nutrients, reducing production costs, and fostering agricultural sustainability, nanofertilizers boost crop yield and quality. According to Kah *et al.*'s (2018) analysis of a dataset of nanofertilizers, nanofertilizers exhibited a median efficacy jump of 18–29% when compared to conventional fertilizers.

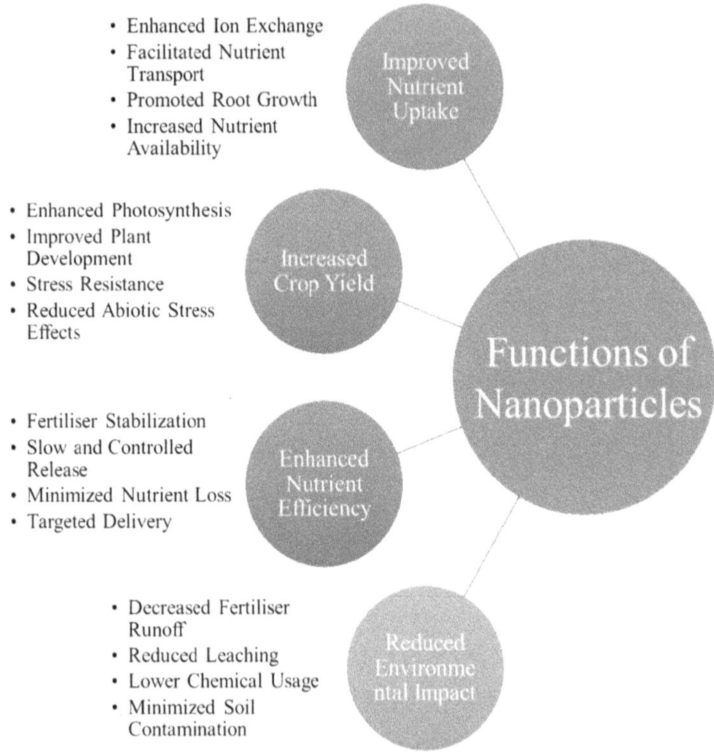

Figure 2: A pictorial explanation of nanoparticle applications.

Phosphoric nanofertilizer treatment has been demonstrated to increase growth rate (by 32%) and seed output (by 20%) when compared to soybean (Glycine max L.) plants treated with conventional fertilizer (Liu and Lal, 2014). Through nanometric apertures made feasible by molecular transporters or nanostructured cuticle holes, nanofertilizers also improve plant metabolism and nutrient absorption, claim Rico *et al.* (2011). Making slow-release or controlled-release fertilizers is made simpler by using nanotechnology to assist plants in acquiring the nutrients they require. These fertilizers increase fertilizer usage efficiency and decrease the quantity of nutrients lost to the environment. They are therefore eco-friendly (Liu and Lal, 2014). Traditional nitrogenous fertilizers have a 30 to 60% efficiency loss in soil owing to chemical bonding, whereas traditional phosphatic fertilizers lose 8 to 90% of their efficacy and become inaccessible to plants (Giroto *et al.*, 2017). Alternatively, after four weeks of incubation, nanocomposites of urea and hydroxyapatite provided regulated nitrogen release, reduced NH3 volatilization, and enhanced phosphorus availability (Giroto *et al.*, 2017). Using slow-release solutions typically results in a reduction in the amount of fertilizer required. In an ideal world, nanofertilizers would release nutrients precisely when and where plants needed them, negating the need to get rid of extra fertilizer through leaching or gasification. According to DeRosa (2010), if nutrients are released in response to signals transmitted from plant roots to soil microbes, then this is possible (Mastronardi *et al.*, 2015). DeRosa (2010) also claims that intelligent fertilizers are now a possibility thanks to an understanding of these signals. Nanomaterials carrying plant nutrients react to a number of chemical and/or physical triggers that indicate the need for nutrients for plant development (DeRosa, 2010). These triggers may include acidification of the rhizosphere and ethylene production by plant roots in response to P and/or K shortages in soils (Rop *et al.*, 2019). According to Syu *et al.*

(2014), using nanoparticles might change internal root signals that affect how much ethylene Arabidopsis roots produce. Internal root triggers for nutrient release in response to P and/or N deficiency may be an important advance for controlled-release nano-fertilizers. Modified NMs can significantly reduce the amount of fertilizer utilized, both in the soil and on the foliage, when compared to normal formulations (Adisa *et al.*, 2019). They become more effective as a result, and their environmental output decreases. Regulatory agencies functioning in many developed nations won't run into any issues as a consequence of their societal acceptance as nano-formulations, according to Kah *et al.* (2019), who researched and supported the use of nano-enabled fertilizers. Nanostructured materials such as clay minerals, hydroxyapatite, chitosan, polyacrylic acid, and zeolite are used to make fertilizers for soil and/or foliar application. Because of the hydroxyapatite's high surface area and robust interactions with it, the release of N from urea occurs slowly (Kottegoda *et al.*, 2011). Urea treated with hydroxyapatite nanoparticles releases nitrogen up to 60 days of plant growth, in contrast to other conventional fertilizers (urea, ammonium nitrate), which release nitrogen only until 30 days of plant development (Kottegoda *et al.*, 2011). Ghafariyan *et al.* (2013) claimed that using superparamagnetic iron oxide boosted the amount of chlorophyll in soybean. A 10% increase in chlorophyll content was discovered in cowpea (Vigna unguiculata (L. Walp.)) by adding Fe nanoparticles to the leaves as a 0.5 g L^{-1} solution and comparing the findings to the same solution of usual forms of Fe (Karami *et al.*, 2014). The growth of the plants was improved in comparison to the control group when mung bean (Vigna radiata (L.) R. Wilczek) and chickpea (Cicer arietinum L.) were treated with 1 and 20 mg L^{-1} ZnO-NP sprays (Mahajan *et al.*, 2011). According to Subbarao *et al.* (2013), polyacrylamide polymer-coated potassium fertilizer has also been discovered to aid in the delayed release of potassium. Slow-release K fertilizers are necessary for sandalwood soils to reduce leaching and K fixation in K-fixing soils. Humic substances (HS), according to Angelico *et al.* (2014) and Usman *et al.* (2018), stabilize colloidal Fe by luring in iron oxides and inhibiting the crystallization of ferric hydroxides. Therefore, Fe-HS composites are used as "nanofertilizer" and coupled with N, P, and K-containing commercial composite fertilizers (Sorkina *et al.*, 2014). The use of HS as macroligands enables enhanced absorption and translocation in plants as well as ecological safety as compared to manufactured iron oxide nanoparticles.

Enhanced organic waste decomposition and compost production may be important applications of nanotechnology in agriculture, but the field of study is very young and no definitive findings have been published so far. According to the information now available, nanofertilizers can reduce the amount of fertilizer that needs to be applied due to their high utilization efficiency, thereby lowering the environmental issues brought on by nutrient losses. This innovation arrives at a critical time for maintaining environmental safety and food security worldwide. Investigating the economic feasibility of nanofertilizers is still important before deploying them in agriculture.

5. Nanobiofertilisers

According to Kole *et al.* (2013), Malusa and Vassilev (2014), Singh *et al.* (2016), and others, biofertilizers are mixtures or products that contain one or more microorganisms that increase soil productivity by fixing nitrogen from the air, making phosphorus more soluble, or assisting plants by producing chemicals that aid in plant growth. So, according to Simarmata *et al.* (2016), nano-biofertilizers are biofertilizers mixed with nanostructures or nanoparticles to promote plant development. Increasing the shelf life of formulations and managing biofertilizer delivery to the soil are essential for attaining this goal.

Some of the most important elements in the creation of nanobiofertilizers are the interaction of nanoparticles and microorganisms, the dispersion of biofertilizers, and their shelf life. According to research (Malusá *et al.*, 2012; Shukla *et al.*, 2015), the interaction between rhizobacteria that aid in plant development and gold nanoparticles has positive outcomes. Silver nanoparticles, on the other hand, cannot be used with biofertilizer because they have detrimental effects on microbial biological processes, such as changing the structure and functions of cell membranes (Duhan *et al.*, 2017). The use of nanoparticles, on the other hand, may increase the shelf life of biofertilizers, which is a limiting factor in these formulations. The use of nanoformulations may make it feasible to increase the stability of biofertilizers in terms of desiccation, heat, and UV inactivation. For example, formulations that are resistant to desiccation may be made using polymeric nanoparticle coatings, extending the useful life of these products (Simarmata *et al.*, 2016; Jamplek and Kráová, 2017).

The delivery of biofertilizers to the soil and plants may also be facilitated by the use of nanomaterials. According to research, hydrophobic silica nanoparticles improve product distribution and increase shelf life by lessening desiccation in water-in-oil emulsions (Kaushik and Djiwanti, 2017). However, because nanoscale structures are often smaller than cells, there is a fundamental issue with the creation of nanobiofertilizers. In this scenario, additional bacteria from fermentation operations might be collected and then introduced to the plants using microscopic screens composed of radially oriented carbon nanotubes that can absorb Escherichia coli (Simarmata *et al.*, 2016; Vandergheynst *et al.*, 2007). The disadvantages of biofertilizers can thus be partially solved by nanobiofertilizers, although this technology still has to be developed and further studied.

According to Kole *et al.* (2013), Malusa and Vassilev (2014), Singh *et al.* (2016), and others, biofertilizers are mixtures or products that contain one or more microorganisms that increase soil productivity by fixing nitrogen from the air, making phosphorus more soluble, or assisting plants by producing chemicals that aid in plant growth. So, according to Simarmata *et al.* (2016), nano-biofertilizers are biofertilizers mixed with nanostructures or nanoparticles to promote plant development. Increasing the shelf life of formulations and managing biofertilizer delivery to the soil are essential for attaining this goal.

6. The drawbacks of nanofertilizers

Undoubtedly, recent developments in sustainable agriculture have enabled the practical use of a variety of nanofertilizers to increase crop output. However, intentionally applying this technology to farming might have several unforeseen and long-lasting implications (Kah, 2015). Unfortunately, extra environmental and unforeseen health and safety issues may prevent this technology from being widely used and, consequently, hinder the development of horticultural crops. Nanomaterial phytotoxicity is a concern in this situation since various plants respond differently to different nanomaterials in a dose-dependent manner (Ashkavand *et al.*, 2018). Therefore, it is crucial to consider both the advantages and disadvantages of nanofertilizers before they are introduced to the market. Nanomaterials are also very reactive due to their incredibly tiny size and enhanced surface area (Konate *et al.*, 2018). The materials' unpredictability and reactivity are also important. This raises safety concerns for agricultural workers since exposure to xenobiotics might occur during their application (Gothandam *et al.*, 2018). These individuals include those who have been exposed to nanofertilizer manufacturing as well as field application. Therefore, in light of the anticipated benefits, it is vital to examine the practicality and usability of these innovative smart fertilizers. Due to serious worries about their transport, toxicity, and bioavailability, as well as unanticipated environmental impacts when exposed to biological systems, they are only appropriate for use in horticulture and sustainable agriculture (Kah, 2015). Setting goals for toxicological research is crucial, as are hazard identification and risk assessment of nanomaterials, including life cycle evaluations of nanomaterials or fertilizers. This is particularly relevant given the buildup of nanoparticles in plants and the associated health hazards. In reality, the use of nanomaterial-based fertilizers has caused grave concerns regarding food security, human health, and safety (López-Moreno *et al.*, 2018; White *et al.*, 2018). According to some studies that have looked at the effects of nanoparticles on plants, species, dose, application method, and NP type (composition, size, shape, and surface features) all play a role in how NPs are absorbed, translocated, transformed, and accumulated (phytotoxicity) in plants (Ebbs *et al.*, 2016).

7. Conclusions and potential outcomes

Nanofertilizers have a significant impact on the agricultural sector in terms of enhanced productivity and resistance to abiotic stresses. Therefore, it is impossible to ignore potential applications for nanofertilizers in the horticulture and agrifood biotechnology sectors. Due to the potential benefits of nanofertilizers, there is also a great deal of interest in increasing the production capacity of agricultural crops in the current climate change scenario. The primary financial benefits of employing nanofertilizers are reduced leaching and volatilization produced by conventional fertilizers. When this technology is employed, the well-known positive impacts on output and product quality have the potential to dramatically increase producers' profit margins. Despite several intriguing outcomes in the field of agriculture, the relevance of nanofertilizers has not yet been focused toward commercial viability. Before commercial distribution of nanofertilizers can start, many unanswered problems concerning how nanomaterials will react in the environment and what impacts they may have on people's health must be resolved. Future research must focus on creating comprehensive knowledge in these uncharted areas in order to develop this new industry of sustainable agriculture.

Research into the toxicity of different nanoparticles used to make nanofertilizers, as well as the security of their use, must thus be given great priority. It is necessary to conduct a thorough analysis of the effects of nanofertilizers in soils with diverse physiochemical properties in order to further recommend a specific nanofertilizer for a certain crop and soil type. Biosynthesized nanoparticle-based fertilizers and nanobiofertilizers should be further studied as a viable way to boost yields while achieving sustainability.

References

1. Adisa, I. O., Pullagurala, V. L. R., Peralta-Videa, J. R., Dimkpa, C. O., Elmer, W. H., Gardea-Torresdey, J. L., and White, J. C. (2019). Recent advances in nano-enabled fertilizers and pesticides: a critical review of mechanisms of action. *Environmental Science: Nano*, 6(7), 2002-2030.
2. Angelico, R., Ceglie, A., He, J. Z., Liu, Y. R., Palumbo, G., and Colombo, C. (2014). Particle size, charge and colloidal stability of humic acids coprecipitated with ferrihydrite. *Chemosphere*, 99, 239-247.
3. Ashkavand, P., Zarafshar, M., Tabari, M., Mirzaie, J., Nikpour, A., Bordbar, S. K., and Striker, G. G. (2018). Application of SiO2 nanoparticles as pretreatment alleviates the impact of drought on the physiological performance of Prunus mahaleb (Rosaceae). *Boletín de la Sociedad Argentina de Botánica*, 53(2), 1-10.
4. Chen, J., and Wei, X. (2018). Controlled-release fertilizers as a means to reduce nitrogen leaching and runoff in container-grown plant production. *Nitrogen in Agriculture-Updates; Khan, A., Fahad, S., Eds*, 33-52.

5. Chhipa, H. (2017). Nanofertilizers and nanopesticides for agriculture. *Environmental chemistry letters*, 15, 15-22.
6. Chhipa, H., and Joshi, P. (2016). Nanofertilisers, nanopesticides and nanosensors in agriculture. *Nanoscience in food and agriculture* 1, 247-282.
7. Cornelis, G., Hund-Rinke, K., Kuhlbusch, T., Van den Brink, N., and Nickel, C. (2014). Fate and bioavailability of engineered nanoparticles in soils: a review. *Critical Reviews in Environmental Science and Technology*, 44(24),2720-2764.
8. DeRosa, M. C., Monreal, C., Schnitzer, M., Walsh, R., and Sultan, Y. (2010). Nanotechnology in fertilizers. *Nature nanotechnology*, *5*(2), 91-91.
9. Dimkpa, C. O., and Bindraban, P. S. (2017). Nanofertilizers: new products for the industry?. *Journal of agricultural and food chemistry*, *66*(26), 6462-6473.
10. Dimkpa, C. O., and Bindraban, P. S. (2017). Nanofertilizers: new products for the industry?. *Journal of agricultural and food chemistry*, *66*(26), 6462-6473.
11. Duhan, J. S., Kumar, R., Kumar, N., Kaur, P., Nehra, K., and Duhan, S. (2017). Nanotechnology: The new perspective in precision agriculture. *Biotechnology Reports*, *15*, 11-23.
12. Ebbs, S. D., Bradfield, S. J., Kumar, P., White, J. C., Musante, C., and Ma, X. (2016). Accumulation of zinc, copper, or cerium in carrot (Daucus carota) exposed to metal oxide nanoparticles and metal ions. *Environmental Science: Nano*, *3*(1), 114-126.

13. El-Ramady, H., Abdalla, N., Alshaal, T., El-Henawy, A., Elmahrouk, M., Bayoumi, Y., ... and Schnug, E. (2018). Plant nano-nutrition: perspectives and challenges. *Nanotechnology, food security and water treatment*, 129-161.
14. Fan, S. (2014, August). Ending hunger and undernutrition by 2025: The role of horticultural value chains. In *XXIX International Horticultural Congress on Horticulture: Sustaining Lives, Livelihoods and Landscapes (IHC2014): Plenary 1126* (pp. 9-20).
15. Feregrino-Perez, A. A., Magaña-López, E., Guzmán, C., and Esquivel, K. (2018). A general overview of the benefits and possible negative effects of the nanotechnology in horticulture. *Scientia Horticulturae, 238*, 126-137.
16. Ghafariyan, M. H., Malakouti, M. J., Dadpour, M. R., Stroeve, P., and Mahmoudi, M. (2013). Effects of magnetite nanoparticles on soybean chlorophyll. *Environmental science and technology*, *47*(18), 10645-10652.
17. Giroto, A. S., Guimarães, G. G., Foschini, M., and Ribeiro, C. (2017). Role of slow-release nanocomposite fertilizers on nitrogen and phosphate availability in soil. *Scientific Reports*, *7*(1), 1-11.
18. Gothandam, K. M., Ranjan, S., Dasgupta, N., Ramalingam, C., and Lichtfouse, E. (Eds.). (2018). *Nanotechnology, food security and water treatment*. Cham: Springer International Publishing.
19. Iavicoli, I., Leso, V., Beezhold, D. H., and Shvedova, A. A. (2017). Nanotechnology in agriculture: Opportunities, toxicological implications, and

occupational risks. *Toxicology and applied pharmacology*, *329*, 96-111.

20. Jampílek, J., and Kráľová, K. (2017). Nanomaterials for delivery of nutrients and growth-promoting compounds to plants. *Nanotechnology: an agricultural paradigm*, 177-226.
21. Kah, M. (2015). Nanopesticides and nanofertilizers: emerging contaminants or opportunities for risk mitigation?. *Frontiers in chemistry*, *3*, 64.
22. Kah, M., Kookana, R. S., Gogos, A., and Bucheli, T. D. (2018). A critical evaluation of nanopesticides and nanofertilizers against their conventional analogues. *Nature nanotechnology*, *13*(8), 677-684.
23. Kah, M., Tufenkji, N., and White, J. C. (2019). Nano-enabled strategies to enhance crop nutrition and protection. *Nature nanotechnology*, *14*(6), 532-540.
24. Karami, M., Bahabadi, M. A., Delfani, S., and Ghozatloo, A. (2014). A new application of carbon nanotubes nanofluid as working fluid of low-temperature direct absorption solar collector. *Solar Energy Materials and Solar Cells*, *121*, 114-118.
25. Kaushik, S., and Djiwanti, S. R. (2017). Nanotechnology for enhancing crop productivity. *Nanotechnology: An Agricultural Paradigm*, 249-262.
26. Kim, D. Y., Kadam, A., Shinde, S., Saratale, R. G., Patra, J., and Ghodake, G. (2018). Recent developments in nanotechnology transforming the agricultural sector: a transition replete with opportunities. *Journal of the Science of Food and Agriculture*, *98*(3), 849-864.

27. Kole, C., Kole, P., Randunu, K. M., Choudhary, P., Podila, R., Ke, P. C., ... and Marcus, R. K. (2013). Nanobiotechnology can boost crop production and quality: first evidence from increased plant biomass, fruit yield and phytomedicine content in bitter melon (Momordica charantia). *BMC biotechnology*, *13*(1), 1-10.
28. Konate, A., Wang, Y., He, X., Adeel, M., Zhang, P., Ma, Y., ... and Zhang, Z. (2018). Comparative effects of nano and bulk-Fe3O4 on the growth of cucumber (Cucumis sativus). *Ecotoxicology and environmental safety*, *165*, 547-554.
29. Kottegoda, N., Munaweera, I., Madusanka, N., and Karunaratne, V. (2011). A green slow-release fertilizer composition based on urea-modified hydroxyapatite nanoparticles encapsulated wood. *Current science*, 73-78.
30. Kyriacou, M. C., and Rouphael, Y. (2018). Towards a new definition of quality for fresh fruits and vegetables. *Scientia Horticulturae*, *234*, 463-469.
31. la, G. N., Pallavi, J., and Shabnam, S. (2015). Nano fertilizers and nano sensors–an attempt for developing smart agriculture. *Int J Eng Res Gen Sci*, *3*(1), 314-320.
32. León-Silva, S., Arrieta-Cortes, R., Fernández-Luqueño, F., and López-Valdez, F. (2018). Design and production of nanofertilizers. *Agricultural Nanobiotechnology: Modern Agriculture for a Sustainable Future*, 17-31.
33. Liu, R., and Lal, R. (2014). Synthetic apatite nanoparticles as a phosphorus fertilizer for soybean (Glycine max). *Scientific reports*, *4*(1), 5686.

34. Liu, R., and Lal, R. (2015). Potentials of engineered nanoparticles as fertilizers for increasing agronomic productions. *Science of the total environment*, *514*, 131-139.
35. López-Moreno, M. L., Cassé, C., and Correa-Torres, S. N. (2018). Engineered NanoMaterials interactions with living plants: Benefits, hazards and regulatory policies. *Current Opinion in Environmental Science and Health*, 6, 36-41.
36. López-Valdez, F., Miranda-Arámbula, M., Ríos-Cortés, A. M., Fernández-Luqueño, F., and de-la-Luz, V. (2018). Nanofertilizers and their controlled delivery of nutrients. *Agricultural Nanobiotechnology: Modern Agriculture for a Sustainable Future*, 35-48.
37. Lu, S., Feng, C., Gao, C., Wang, X., Xu, X., Bai, X., ... and Liu, M. (2016). Multifunctional environmental smart fertilizer based on L-aspartic acid for sustained nutrient release. *Journal of agricultural and food chemistry*, *64*(24), 4965-4974.
38. Ma, C., White, J. C., Zhao, J., Zhao, Q., and Xing, B. (2018). Uptake of engineered nanoparticles by food crops: characterization, mechanisms, and implications. *Annual review of food science and technology*, *9*, 129-153.
39. Mahajan, P., Dhoke, S. K., and Khanna, A. S. (2011). Effect of nano-ZnO particle suspension on growth of mung (Vigna radiata) and gram (Cicer arietinum) seedlings using plant agar method. *Journal of Nanotechnology*, *2011*.
40. Malusa, E., and Vassilev, N. (2014). A contribution to set a legal framework for biofertilisers. *Applied microbiology and biotechnology*, *98*, 6599-6607.

41. Malusá, E., Sas-Paszt, L., and Ciesielska, J. J. T. S. W. J. (2012). Technologies for beneficial microorganisms inocula used as biofertilizers. *The scientific world journal, 2012.*
42. Mastronardi, E., Tsae, P., Zhang, X., Monreal, C., and DeRosa, M. C. (2015). Strategic role of nanotechnology in fertilizers: potential and limitations. *Nanotechnologies in food and agriculture*, 25-67.
43. Monreal, C. M., DeRosa, M., Mallubhotla, S. C., Bindraban, P. S., and Dimkpa, C. (2016). Nanotechnologies for increasing the crop use efficiency of fertilizer-micronutrients. *Biology and fertility of soils*, *52*, 423-437.
44. Parisi, C., Vigani, M., and Rodríguez-Cerezo, E. (2015). Agricultural nanotechnologies: what are the current possibilities?. *Nano Today*, *10*(2), 124-127.
45. Prasad, R., Bhattacharyya, A., and Nguyen, Q. D. (2017). Nanotechnology in sustainable agriculture: recent developments, challenges, and perspectives. *Frontiers in microbiology*, *8*, 1014.
46. Raliya, R., and Tarafdar, J. C. (2013). ZnO nanoparticle biosynthesis and its effect on phosphorous-mobilizing enzyme secretion and gum contents in Clusterbean (Cyamopsis tetragonoloba L.). *Agricultural Research*, *2*, 48-57.
47. Raliya, R., Biswas, P., and Tarafdar, J. C. (2015). TiO2 nanoparticle biosynthesis and its physiological effect on mung bean (Vigna radiata L.). *Biotechnology Reports*, *5*, 22-26.
48. Raliya, R., Saharan, V., Dimkpa, C., and Biswas, P. (2017). Nanofertilizer for precision and sustainable

agriculture: current state and future perspectives. *Journal of agricultural and food chemistry*, *66*(26), 6487-6503.

49. Raliya, R., Tarafdar, J. C., and Biswas, P. (2016). Enhancing the mobilization of native phosphorus in the mung bean rhizosphere using ZnO nanoparticles synthesized by soil fungi. *Journal of agricultural and food chemistry*, *64*(16), 3111-3118.
50. Rico, C. M., Majumdar, S., Duarte-Gardea, M., Peralta-Videa, J. R., and Gardea-Torresdey, J. L. (2011). Interaction of nanoparticles with edible plants and their possible implications in the food chain. *Journal of agricultural and food chemistry*, *59*(8), 3485-3498.
51. Rop, K., Karuku, G. N., Mbui, D., Njomo, N., and Michira, I. (2019). Evaluating the effects of formulated nano-NPK slow release fertilizer composite on the performance and yield of maize, kale and capsicum. *Annals of Agricultural Sciences*, *64*(1), 9-19.
52. Shukla, S. K., Kumar, R., Mishra, R. K., Pandey, A., Pathak, A., Zaidi, M. G. H., ... and Dikshit, A. (2015). Prediction and validation of gold nanoparticles (GNPs) on plant growth promoting rhizobacteria (PGPR): a step toward development of nano-biofertilizers. *Nanotechnology Reviews*, *4*(5), 439-448.
53. Simarmata, T., Turmuktini, T., Fitriatin, B. N., and Setiawati, M. R. (2016). Application of bioameliorant and biofertilizers to increase the soil health and rice productivity. *HAYATI Journal of Biosciences*, *23*(4), 181-184.

54. Singh, H. B., Sarma, B. K., and Keswani, C. (2016). *Agriculturally important microorganisms*. Singapore: Springer.
55. Solanki, P., Bhargava, A., Chhipa, H., Jain, N., and Panwar, J. (2015). Nano-fertilizers and their smart delivery system. *Nanotechnologies in food and agriculture*, 81-101.
56. Sorkina, T. A., Polyakov, A. Y., Kulikova, N. A., Goldt, A. E., Philippova, O. I., Aseeva, A. A., ... and Perminova, I. V. (2014). Nature-inspired soluble iron-rich humic compounds: new look at the structure and properties. *Journal of soils and sediments*, *14*, 261-268.
57. Srivastava, A. K., and Malhotra, S. K. (2017). Nutrient use efficiency in perennial fruit crops—A review. *Journal of Plant Nutrition*, *40*(13), 1928-1953.
58. Subbarao, C. V., Kartheek, G., and Sirisha, D. (2013). Slow release of potash fertilizer through polymer coating. *International Journal of Applied science and engineering*, *11*(1), 25-30.
59. Syu, Y. Y., Hung, J. H., Chen, J. C., and Chuang, H. W. (2014). Impacts of size and shape of silver nanoparticles on Arabidopsis plant growth and gene expression. *Plant physiology and biochemistry*, *83*, 57-64.
60. Tan, W., Du, W., Barrios, A. C., Armendariz Jr, R., Zuverza-Mena, N., Ji, Z., ... and Gardea-Torresdey, J. L. (2017). Surface coating changes the physiological and biochemical impacts of nano-TiO2 in basil (Ocimum basilicum) plants. *Environmental Pollution*, *222*, 64-72.
61. Usman, M., Byrne, J. M., Chaudhary, A., Orsetti, S., Hanna, K., Ruby, C., ... and Haderlein, S. B. (2018).

Magnetite and green rust: synthesis, properties, and environmental applications of mixed-valent iron minerals. *Chemical reviews*, *118*(7), 3251-3304.

62. Van Eerd, L. L., Turnbull, J. J. D., Bakker, C. J., Vyn, R. J., McKeown, A. W., and Westerveld, S. M. (2017). Comparing soluble to controlled-release nitrogen fertilizers: storage cabbage yield, profit margins, and N use efficiency. *Canadian Journal of Plant Science*, *98*(4), 815-829.
63. Vandergheynst, J., Scher, H., Guo, H. Y., and Schultz, D. (2007). Water-in-oil emulsions that improve the storage and delivery of the biolarvacide Lagenidium giganteum. *BioControl*, *52*, 207-229.
64. White, J. C., and Gardea-Torresdey, J. (2018). Achieving food security through the very small. *Nature nanotechnology*, *13*(8), 627-629.
65. Zuverza-Mena, N., Martínez-Fernández, D., Du, W., Hernandez-Viezcas, J. A., Bonilla-Bird, N., López-Moreno, M. L., ... and Gardea-Torresdey, J. L. (2017). Exposure of engineered nanomaterials to plants: Insights into the physiological and biochemical responses-A review. *Plant Physiology and Biochemistry*, *110*, 236-264.

2.

FROM PLANT TO PLATE: UNDERSTANDING THE BENEFITS OF DIETARY FIBRES ON HEALTH

Dr. Harish Rangareddy, Assistant Professor, Department of Biochemistry, Haveri Institute of Medical Sciences, Haveri, Karnataka-581110

Mrs. Anitha Misquith, Assistant Professor, Department of Biochemistry, Sapthagiri Institute of Medical Sciences & Research Center, Bengaluru, Karnataka-560090

Dr. Ashakiran Srinivasaiah, Professor and Head, Department of Biochemistry, Haveri Institute of Medical Sciences, Haveri, Karnataka-581110

Dr. Achal Shetty, Assistant Professor, Department of Community Medicine, Father Muller Medical College, Mangalore, Karnataka-575002

Email: harishreddy1349@gmail.com

Abstract

Dietary Fibres are recognized as essential components of a balanced healthy diet, playing a pivotal role in promoting optimal health and preventing a range of diseases. Dietary fiber denotes the indigestible components of foods from plant origin, primarily derived from carbohydrates. A wide range of foods contain dietary fiber, viz. vegetables, pulses, whole grains, nuts, fruits and seeds are high in fiber content. To ensure an adequate intake of different types of dietary fiber and the health benefits associated with it our diet must include a variety of these foods in the diet. This chapter provides a comprehensive representation of the dietary fibers, encompassing their definition, types, and the extensive health benefits they offer. One of the primary benefits of dietary fiber is its positive impact on the digestive system. It prevents constipation by promoting regular bowel movements and facilitates maintaining a healthy gastrointestinal system. Fibre adds bulk to the stool, facilitating its smooth passage through the intestines. Dietary fibers are critical for weight management by increasing the satiety and reducing overall calorie intake. Soluble dietary fibers slow down the absorption of glucose into the bloodstream, promoting stable postprandial blood glucose levels. This function of fibers is helpful in controlling glycemic variability in individuals with diabetes mellitus. Consumption of an adequate quantity of dietary fiber has been linked with lowered cardiovascular disease risk due to cholesterol-lowering properties. Dietary fiber serves as prebiotic, providing nourishment for beneficial bacteria in the gut. A diverse and healthy gut microbiome is associated with improved immune function, reduced inflammation, and better overall health. By comprehending the multifaceted benefits of dietary fibers, individuals are empowered to make informed choices that can enhance their overall well-being, mitigate the risk of disease, and cultivate a healthier lifestyle.

Keywords: digestive system, colon cancer, cardiovascular disease, metabolism

1. Introduction

Diet has a fundamental role in the overall health and well-being of an individual, with various components contributing to the complex interplay between nutrition and disease prevention. Among these components, dietary fibers hold a significant place due to their remarkable impact on our health. Dietary fibers found abundantly in plant-based foods have emerged as essential elements of a balanced diet that promote digestive health, weight management, and the prevention of chronic illness.

This chapter explores the definition of dietary fibers, their classification, and the overarching significance of these fibers in maintaining optimal health and preventing various diseases.

The historical interest in dietary fiber can be traced back to Hippocrates, who first highlighted the laxative effects of coarse wheat (Hijová, E., Bertková, I., & Štofilová, J. 2019). During the 1920s, Kellogg's publications generated increased fascination with dietary fiber by highlighting its various benefits, such as promoting bowel movements, increasing stool bulk, and preventing diseases (Slavin J. L., 1987). In the mid-20th century, the importance of dietary fiber received less attention. However, it regained significance in the 1970s due to the influential works of Burkitt D. P. (1971). Burkitt's publication suggested the protective effects of dietary fiber against conditions like colonic cancer, diabetes mellitus, and obesity. Subsequently, further studies have advanced our knowledge of the numerous advantages associated with dietary fiber, leading to a better appreciation of its health benefits (Burkitt D., 1991).

Unlike other macronutrients such as proteins, fats, and carbohydrates, dietary fibers resist enzymatic breakdown in the human digestive system. They pass through the gastrointestinal tract intact, exerting unique physiological effects along the way. By providing bulk to the diet, dietary fibers play a crucial role in maintaining regular bowel movements, preventing constipation, and supporting a healthy digestive system (Barber, T. M., Kabisch, S., Pfeiffer, A. F. H., & Weickert, M. O., 2020).

Dietary fibers typically encompass two main types:

i. soluble fibres

ii. insoluble fibres

Soluble fibers form a viscous gel-like substance in the digestive tract when dissolved in water. They can be found in foods such as oats, legumes, citrus fruits, and apples. Insoluble fibers add bulk to the stool, facilitating its passage through the intestines. Whole grains, vegetables and nuts are common sources of insoluble fibers. Both types of fibers offer unique benefits to human health and serve as vital components of a well-rounded diet (Barber, T. M. et al., 2020).

Extensively studied and linked to various health benefits, the impact of dietary fiber on health goes beyond their role in digestion. Their ability to promote weight management has been recognized, as fiber rich foods increase satiety, aiding in appetite control and potentially reducing calorie intake. By slowing down the intestinal absorption of glucose into the bloodstream, certain soluble fibers assist in blood sugar control, making them beneficial for individuals with diabetes mellitus (Dhingra, D., Michael, M., Rajput, H., & Patil, R. T., 2012).

In addition to their positive impact on the circulatory system, dietary fibers have been found to lower total cholesterol by binding bile salts and preventing absorption of cholesterol in the intestine. This cholesterol-lowering effect can contribute to a reduced risk of cardiovascular diseases. Additionally, fiber-rich diets have been associated with improved lipid profiles and a decreased likelihood of developing heart disease. This chapter reconnoitres the specific health benefits, food sources and role of dietary fibers in various health conditions and provide practical recommendations for incorporating them into our daily lives (Dhingra, D. et al., 2012).

2. Definition and types of dietary fibres

Originally, the term "fiber" encompassed plant components that were resistant to the activity of human digestive enzymes, including substances such as lignin and polysaccharides. However, the definition was subsequently expanded to encompass additional substances like resistant starches, inulin, and other oligosaccharides. It is worth noting that the exact definition of dietary fiber may vary slightly across different institutions.

Organization	Definition
American Association of Cereal Chemists	“Dietary fibre is the edible parts of plant or analogous carbohydrates that are resistant to digestion and absorption in the human small intestine with complete

(AACC)., 2000	or partial fermentation in the large intestine. Dietary fibre includes polysaccharides, oligosaccharides, lignin and associated plant substances".
Australia New Zealand Food Authority (ANZFA)., 2001	"Dietary fibre is that "fraction of the edible part of plants or their extracts, or analogous carbohydrates, that are resistant to digestion and absorption in the human small intestine, usually with complete or partial fermentation in the large intestine. The term includes polysaccharides, oligosaccharides and lignins".
National Academy of Science., 2002	"Dietary fibre complex includes "dietary fibre consisting of non-digestible carbohydrates and lignin that are intrinsic and intact in plants, functional fibres consisting of isolated, non-digestible carbohydrates which have beneficial physiological effects in humans and total fibre as the sum of dietary fibre and functional fibre" (Trumbo, P., Schlicker, S., Yates, A. A., & Poos, M. et al., 2002).

The classification of carbohydrates is based on their number of carbohydrate moieties. Monosaccharides and most oligosaccharides, which consist of 1-2 monomers and 3-9 monomers respectively, can be digested. On the other hand, polysaccharides like cellulose with 10 or more monomers are typically indigestible owing to the lack of enzyme cellulase. Although considered a type of carbohydrate, dietary fiber is defined by its non-digestibility, which is attributed to the beta-acetyl linkage (Tungland, B. C., & Meyer, D., 2002). European Food Safety Authority (EFSA) defines the dietary fiber as "non-digestible carbohydrates along with lignin". EFSA provides a comprehensive list of substances that are classified as dietary fiber, which includes cellulose, pectins, hydrocolloids, non-starch polysaccharides, resistant starch and fructo-oligosaccharides. (Hijova E et al., 2019).

As stated previously, dietary fibers are classified based on their solubility in water. Soluble fiber is primarily found in vegetables and fruits, whereas cereals and whole-grain products are significant sources of insoluble fiber. It is important to note that most high-fiber foods naturally contain varying amounts of both soluble and insoluble fiber. While gut microbiota to a lesser extent ferment most dietary fiber within the gastrointestinal tract, soluble fiber tends to undergo fermentation more readily when compared to insoluble fiber from cereals (Barber, T. M. et al., 2020).

Gastrointestinal tract is influenced by dietary fiber through its ability to modify the contents within and affect the absorption of other nutrients and chemicals. Specific types of soluble fiber have the characteristic of forming a gel-like substance when combined with water and undergo fermentation by bacteria present in the digestive tract. In contrast, some types of insoluble fiber provide bulk but are not fermented. Lignin, which is a significant contributor to insoluble fiber in the diet, may impact the rate and metabolism of soluble fibers. On the other hand, resistant starch which is also an insoluble fiber undergoes complete fermentation (Fuentes-Zaragoza, E., Riquelme-Navarrete, M. J., Sánchez-Zapata, E., & Pérez-Álvarez, J. A. et al., 2010).

Plant-based foods contain varying amounts of both types of dietary fibers, depending on the characteristics of the specific plant. From a chemical perspective, dietary fiber is composed of non-starch polysaccharides, including cellulose, arabinoxylans, resistant dextrins, resistant starch, inulin, lignin, pectins, beta-glucans, waxes, chitins and oligosaccharides (Mudgil, D., 2017).

Advantages of dietary fiber consumption include the production of beneficial compounds during the soluble fiber fermentation and the increased bulk with softened stool by action the insoluble dietary fibers leading to shortened transit time in the intestinal tract due to its hygroscopic properties. However, a high-fiber diet can have drawbacks. It may lead to significant flatulence and bloating in some individuals. Additionally, if an adequate amount of fluids is not consumed alongside a high-fiber diet, it can result in constipation. Absorption of dietary micronutrients may also be impaired.

3. Specific dietary fiber components found in food sources

3.1. Cellulose

Cellulose, an insoluble fiber, is present abundantly in plant cell walls. It provides structural support to plants and is found in various vegetables, fruits, legumes, and whole grains. Foods such as broccoli, Brussels sprouts, leafy greens, and whole wheat products are good sources of cellulose. These foods promote regular bowel movements and aid in digestive health by adding bulk to the stool(Khalid, W.,

Arshad, M. S., Jabeen, A., Muhammad Anjum, F., Qaisrani, T. B., & Suleria, H. A. R., 2022).

Cellulose, a fundamental component of plant cell walls, comprises glucose units connected by β-1,4 glucosidic bonds in a linear chain arrangement. Its structural integrity, resilience against degradation, low solubility in water, and resistance to acid hydrolysis are ascribed to the presence of hydrogen bonding within microfibrils. While cellulose remains insoluble in potent alkalis, a fraction (10-15%) referred to as "amorphous" exhibits increased susceptibility to acid hydrolysis. Enzymes in the human gastrointestinal system do not significantly digest cellulose (Aspinall, G. O., 1980).

Unlike cellulose, hemicellulose is a collective term for a group of polysaccharides found in cell walls that can be rendered soluble through treatment with aqueous alkali, following the removal of water-soluble and pectic polysaccharides. These polysaccharides, comprising glucose units connected by β-1,4 glucosidic bonds, display variations in terms of size, sugar composition, and branching when compared to cellulose. Hemicellulose contains primarily xylose, along with some mannose, galactose, arabinose and other sugars (Kay R. M., 1982).

3.2. Pectin

Pectin is a soluble fiber commonly found in fruits, especially citrus fruits, apples, and berries. It is also present in some vegetables like carrots and potatoes. Pectin forms a gel-like substance when combined with water, helps in regulating bowel movements and can contribute to lowering cholesterol levels (Lara-Espinoza, C., Carvajal-Millán, E.,

Balandrán-Quintana, R., López-Franco, Y., & Rascón-Chu, A., 2018).

D-galacturonic acid is a primary constituent of pectin polysaccharides. It serves as a structural component of plant cell walls and acts as an intercellular adhesive. Pectin is exceedingly water-soluble and the colonic bacteria metabolize most of it. The gel-forming characteristics of pectin have the potential to reduce the pace of gastric emptying and impact the duration of transit within the small intestine. These characteristics contribute to its hypoglycemic properties (Lara-Espinoza, C. et al., 2018).

3.3. Lignin

Lignin is a complex, insoluble fiber found in the woody parts of plants. It is abundant in whole grains, vegetables like broccoli and asparagus, and some fruits like pears. Lignin adds roughage to the diet, aiding in maintaining regular bowel movements. Though lignin is integral part of dietary fiber composition it is not fermented by colonic bacteria (Wrick, K. L. F., 1979).

While not classified as a polysaccharide, lignin is a complex polymer consisting of around 40 oxygenated phenylpropane units, such as sinapyl, coniferyl and p-coumaric alcohols. It undergoes intricate dehydrogenative polymerization. Lignins display variations in molecular weight and methoxyl content. Lignin demonstrates significant inertness and remarkable resistance in comparison to other naturally-occurring polymers due to robust intramolecular bonding which including carbon-carbon linkages (Theander, O., Aman, P., 1979).

3.4. Gum and Mucilages

Gum and mucilages are types of soluble fiber that form viscous gels when mixed with water. They are commonly found in certain plant seeds and legumes, such as flaxseeds, chia seeds, and lentils. These fibers can help regulate blood sugar levels and contribute to a feeling of fullness. Gum and mucilages also aid in maintaining healthy cholesterol levels and promoting gut health (Cruz-Rubio, J. M., Loeppert, R., Viernstein, H., & Praznik, W., 2018).

Gums and mucilages are produced within specialized secretory cells of plants which differ from cell wall components. They are highly branched polysaccharides that have the ability to form gels and exhibit water-binding properties. Gums are adhesive substances that are released in response to plant injury, such as gum arabic. Guar gum and gum arabic serve as notable examples of gums. Guar gum is a galactomannan derived from the seeds of Cyamopsis tetragonolobus (guar). When guar gum undergoes partial enzymatic hydrolysis, it yields a soluble dietary fiber. The physiological effects of this fiber align with the expected outcomes of soluble fiber consumption. On the other hand, gum arabic is obtained as an exudate from the acacia tree and consists of a complex arabinogalactan polysaccharide in conjunction with a glycoprotein (Van Denffer, D., Schumacher, W., Magdefrau, K., Ehrendorfer, F., 1976).

4. Dietary fibres and specific health conditions

A renewed scientific interest in dietary fiber was noticed in the 1970s, largely influenced by the research of Dr. Denis P.

Burkitt (1973). Since then, a significant body of scientific evidence has accumulated, shedding light on the consumption of dietary fiber and various health benefits associated.

4.1. Gut motility and Constipation

Insoluble fiber is essential for promoting regular and healthy bowel movements while preventing constipation. It possesses the capacity to absorb water, aiding in the softening of stools and facilitating smoother bowel movements.

Researchers who investigated the impact of dietary fiber on bowel function in healthy individuals found that an increased intake of in insoluble fiber led to an increase in stool weight, frequency, indicating improved bowel movements and a reduced risk of constipation (Cummings et al., 1992). Additionally, insoluble fiber increases stool bulk, prevents the formation of loose stools, implying that an increase in insoluble fiber intake resulted in firmer stools, reducing the likelihood of diarrhea (Müller-Lissner, S. A., Kamm, M. A., Scarpignato, C., & Wald, A., 2005).

A randomized control trial investigated the association between dietary fiber consumption and possibility of symptomatic hemorrhoids. The trial results demonstrated that individuals with higher fiber intake had a considerably decreased risk of developing hemorrhoids compared to those with lower fiber intake (Ho, Y. H., Tan, M., & Seow-Choen, F., 2000).

Similarly, a cohort study prospectively examined the association between dietary fiber intake and the development of diverticular disease. The results of the study indicated that an increased intake of dietary fiber was linked to a reduced risk of diverticular disease. These findings suggest that fiber plays a protective role in preventing the development of this condition (Crowe, F. L., Appleby, P. N., Allen, N. E., & Key, T. J., 2011).

4.2. Gut microflora and metabolites

The gut microbiota, comprised of an estimated 100 trillion microbes, has co-evolved with our hominid ancestors over millions of years. Our understanding of the gut microbiota has undergone a significant transformation recently. A diverse and healthy gut microbiota is crucial for normal physiological functions, encompassing metabolic pathways, immune development and even mental well-being. On the other hand, discrepancies in the gut microbiota, known as "gut dysbiosis", are associated with many chronic illnesses of the 21st century. These imbalances can disrupt chronic inflammatory pathways, impair immune function, and contribute to conditions such as atopy, food intolerances, and autoimmune disorders (Opoku-Acheampong, I., McLaud, T., & Anderson, O. S., 2022).

Fortunately, the composition of our gut microbiota can be modified through lifestyle factors, primarily through our dietary choices. By improving our gut flora, we can enhance our future prospects for good health. One effective approach to attain this is by optimizing our dietary intake of fiber. The understanding of how dietary fiber influences the gut microbiota and its impact on overall health primarily stems from studies conducted on rodents. These investigations have specifically examined the effects of dietary fiber intake on colonic health (Cronin, P., Joyce, S. A., O'Toole, P. W., & O'Connor, E. M., 2021).

For instance, a study utilizing a "gnotobiotic" mouse model, where human gut microbiota were used to colonize mice, demonstrated that chronic deficiency in dietary fiber led to the gut microbiota utilizing mucus glycoproteins secreted by the host as an alternative nutrient source. This resulted in the destruction of the colonic mucus barrier, increased vulnerability to pathogenic bacterial invasion and a higher susceptibility to severe colitis (Desai M.S. et al., 2016).

Dietary fibers interact directly with our gut microbes and promote the production of an important microbial metabolite which has significant effects on our overall health and well-being - short-chain fatty acids (SCFAs).

Rodent studies have demonstrated that short-chain fatty acids (SCFAs) can impact gut motility, suppress appetite by increasing the release of incretins such as glucagon-like peptide-1 (GLP-1), and enhance insulin sensitivity (Li, Z. et al., 2018). Human studies have provided further evidence supporting the beneficial effects of short-chain fatty acids (SCFAs), including the role of propionate—a common SCFA produced by the human gut microbiota. Propionate has been found to enhance incretin response, promote weight loss, reduce volume of intra-abdominal adipose tissue and intra-hepatocellular lipid content, and preserve insulin sensitivity. The underlying mechanisms of these effects involve interactions within the gut microbiota-brain axis, specifically through the release of by-products from gut microbes such as secondary bile acids, tryptophan metabolites and SCFAs. These compounds are capable of communicating with various components, including enteroendocrine cells, enterochromaffin cells and the mucosal immune system. Short-chain fatty acids (SCFAs) can potentially penetrate blood-brain barrier, influencing the hypothalamic control of metabolic pathways and appetite directly. (Chambers, E. S. et al., 2015).

Dietary fibers interaction with gut microbes influences microbial ecology and promotes the production of SCFAs, which have wide-ranging effects on metabolic processes and overall health. While SCFAs play a significant role in mediating these effects, other factors associated with dietary fiber, such as insoluble cereal fibers and their impact on fecal bulk and microbial mass, may also contribute to the observed metabolic benefits. Additional investigation is necessary to comprehensively understand the intricate mechanisms that govern the connection between dietary fiber, gut microbiota, and metabolic well-being.

4.3. Colorectal cancer

A high consumption of dietary fiber, particularly derived from fruits, whole grains, vegetables, and pulses, has consistently shown a decreased risk of developing colorectal cancer. A meta-analysis conducted confirmed a significant inverse relationship between dietary fiber intake and the risk of colorectal cancer. The analysis demonstrated that with every 10 grams per day increment in fiber intake, there was a corresponding 10% reduction in the risk of developing colorectal cancer (Aune, D., Chan, D. S., Lau, R., Vieira, R., Greenwood, D. C., Kampman, E., & Norat, T., 2011).

Another meta-analysis further supported the protecting effect of dietary fiber against colorectal cancer. This meta-analysis revealed that a high intake of dietary fiber, particularly whole grain and cereals, was related with lowered incidence of colorectal cancer (Ben, Q., Sun, Y., Chai, R., Qian, A., Xu, B., & Yuan, Y., 2014).

A multicentric study investigated the association between colorectal cancer risk and decreased dietary fiber intake. The study found a reduced risk of colorectal cancer to be associated with increased intake of soluble fiber, specifically from vegetables and fruits (Murphy N. et al., 2012).

The existing literature available on PubMed consistently reinforces the notion that a high consumption of dietary fiber, particularly obtained from whole grains, fruits, vegetables, and legumes, is correlated with a reduced risk of colorectal cancer. The evidence strongly indicates that increasing fiber intake, particularly from a variety of sources, can contribute to the prevention of colorectal cancer and its precursor lesions. Including a fiber-rich diet as part of a healthy lifestyle may prove advantageous in mitigating the risk of developing colorectal cancer.

The protective effects of dietary fiber against colorectal cancer can be attributed to several factors. These include increased frequency of bowel movements, which helps eliminate carcinogens, as well as the binding and dilution of these harmful substances. Additionally, dietary fiber promotes the production of short-chain fatty acids (SCFAs) and modulates the gut microbiota. Furthermore, it improves insulin sensitivity, which may further contribute to its protective role against colorectal cancer. Nevertheless, it is essential to conduct additional research to fully comprehend the underlying mechanisms and establish causal relationships between the dietary fiber consumption and the prevention of colorectal cancer (Biswas, V., Praveen, A.,

Mariotti, A. L., Sharma, A., Kumar, V., Sahu, S. K., & Tewari, D., 2022).

4.4. Chronic inflammation

Dietary fibers exhibit a significant role in modulating chronic inflammation, and several studies available on PubMed have investigated this relationship. Lowered levels of inflammatory markers have been associated with sufficient intake of dietary fiber. The association between dietary fiber intake and markers of systemic inflammation has been explored in a large population-based cohort study which unraveled a negative association between increased fiber intake and inflammatory markers viz., interleukin-6 (IL-6) and C-reactive protein (CRP) (Grooms, K. N., Ommerborn, M. J., Pham, D. Q., Djoussé, L., & Clark, C. R., 2013).

Dietary fiber can alter the composition of the gut microbiota which in turn influences the inflammatory status of the host. A study published in Nature Communications investigated the impact of dietary fiber on gut microbiota and immune response in mice. The study provided evidence that dietary fiber stimulated the proliferation of beneficial bacteria, such as Lactobacillus & Bifidobacterium, while inhibiting the growth of pro-inflammatory bacteria. As a result, this led to a decrease in intestinal inflammation (Queiroz-Monici, K. D. S., Costa, G. E., da Silva, N., Reis, S. M., & de Oliveira, A. C., 2005).

Short-chain fatty acids (SCFAs) produced by gut microbial fermentation of dietary fiber, have anti-inflammatory properties. They can modulate immune responses and inhibit the formation of pro-inflammatory cytokines. A review published in Frontiers in Immunology discussed the immunomodulatory effects of SCFAs, highlighting their ability to regulate inflammation in the gut and systemically (Tang, M., Li, S., Wei, L., Hou, Z., Qu, J., & Li, L., 2021).

Dietary fiber consumption can contribute to maintaining the integrity of the gut barrier, which serves as a protective shield against the translocation of bacteria and their by-products into the systemic circulation. Increased fiber intake improves gut barrier integrity, as indicated by reduced plasma lipopolysaccharide (LPS), a marker of bacterial translocation (Vijay, A., & Valdes, A. M., 2022).

In a study published in Diabetes Care which investigated the association between intake dietary fiber and markers of adipose tissue inflammation in overweight and obese individuals; it was observed that higher fiber intake was associated with decreased adipose tissue inflammation markers, including adiponectin and leptin (Parikh, S., Pollock, N. K., Bhagatwala, J., Guo, D. H., Gutin, B., Zhu, H., & Dong, Y., 2012).

Chronic inflammation may be attenuated by dietary fibres through various mechanisms, including the reduction of inflammatory markers, gut microbiota modulation, gut barrier preservation, anti-inflammatory SCFA production and adipose tissue inflammation reduction. Including a fiber-rich diet as a component of a healthy lifestyle has the potential to alleviate chronic inflammation and mitigate the accompanying health risks.

4.5. Cardiovascular disease

The role of dietary fibers in reducing the risk of cardiovascular disease is characterized by their active involvement in lowering cholesterol levels.

Reduction of LDL Cholesterol: Dietary fibers aid cardiovascular health primarily by reducing low-density lipoprotein (LDL) cholesterol levels. A meta-analysis studying the impact of dietary fiber supplementation on blood lipid levels revealed that higher intake of dietary fiber, especially soluble fiber, significantly lowered LDL cholesterol levels (Brown, L., Rosner, B., Willett, W. W., & Sacks, F. M., 1999).

Modulation of Bile Acid Metabolism: Dietary fibers have the ability to impact bile acid metabolism, which is crucial for maintaining cholesterol balance. A study published in the Journal of Nutrition examined the effects of dietary fiber on bile acid metabolism in hamsters which revealed that higher intake of soluble fiber resulted in improved excretion of bile acids and reduced levels of cholesterol in the bloodstream (Tong, L. T., Zhong, K., Liu, L., Qiu, J., Guo, L., Zhou, X., Cao, L., & Zhou, S., 2014).

Viscous Fibre and Cholesterol Reduction: Viscous or soluble fibers present in psyllium and oats viz., beta-glucan has been explored for its cholesterol-lowering effects. In a systematic review with meta-analysis of the effects of incorporating viscous fiber supplementation on blood lipid levels demonstrated a significant reduction of LDL cholesterol and total cholesterol with consumption of viscous fibers (Reynolds, A. N., Akerman, A., Kumar, S., Diep Pham, H. T., Coffey, S., & Mann, J., 2022).

Impact on Lipoprotein Particle Size: Favorable changes in lipoprotein particle size linked to reduced cardiovascular risk has been observed with consumption of adequate dietary fibers (Millar, S. R., Navarro, P., Harrington, J. M., Shivappa, N., Hébert, J. R., Perry, I. J., & Phillips, C. M., 2021).

Cardiovascular Disease Risk Reduction: Several prospective cohort studies have examined the potential link between dietary fiber intake and cardiovascular disease risk. Among these, a study published in the Archives of Internal Medicine analyzed data from the National Institutes of Health (NIH)-AARP Diet and Health Study. The results demonstrated that individuals who consumed higher amounts of dietary fiber had a reduced risk of developing cardiovascular disease and stroke. (Park, Y., Subar, A. F., Hollenbeck, A., & Schatzkin, A., 2011).

Collectively, these studies provide evidence that dietary fibers, specifically soluble fibers, possess cholesterol-lowering properties and play a significant role in reducing the risk of cardiovascular disease. Including fiber-rich foods like fruits, vegetables, whole grains, and legumes in the diet is essential for maintaining cardiovascular health.

4.6. Metabolic health and Insulin sensitivity

Soluble fibers have a significant role in regulating postprandial glucose levels and improving insulin sensitivity in the body. The effect of soluble fibers on carbohydrate metabolism and insulin response has been explored in several studies.

Soluble fibers have the ability to form viscous gels when mixed with water. The gel-like texture of soluble fibers in the gastrointestinal tract leads to a deceleration in the digestion and absorption of carbohydrates. Consumption of soluble fibers like guar gum or pectin notably delays the absorption of glucose, resulting in a reduced postprandial blood glucose response (Jenkins, D. J., Leeds, A. R., Gassull, M. A., Cochet, B., & Alberti, G. M., 1977).

By slowing down carbohydrate absorption, soluble fibers help to stabilize postprandial glucose levels. This leads to a reduced demand for insulin, as the body can more effectively manage the influx of glucose. A randomized controlled trial published in Diabetes Care examined the impact of soluble fiber supplementation on postprandial glucose response and insulin demand in individuals with type 2 diabetes. The study revealed that the consumption of soluble fibers, such as psyllium husk, resulted in improved glucose regulation and reduced insulin demand (de Carvalho, C. M., de Paula, T. P., Viana, L. V., Machado, V. M., de Almeida, J. C., & Azevedo, M. J., 2017).

Dietary fibers consumption has been linked with enhanced insulin sensitivity, which is crucial for maintaining healthy blood glucose levels. Higher intake of dietary fiber associated with improved insulin sensitivity in this population has been evidenced in a systematic review and meta-analysis (Mao, T., Huang, F., Zhu, X., Wei, D., & Chen, L., 2021).

Soluble dietary fibers play a crucial role in regulating postprandial glucose levels, reducing insulin demand, and improving insulin sensitivity. By slowing carbohydrate absorption, soluble fibers benefit individuals with diabetes or those at risk of developing metabolic disorders.

5. Recommendations for fibre intake

A high-fiber diet can be defined as a dietary pattern that meets or exceeds the recommended intake of dietary fiber established by the United States Institute of Medicine (IOM). The current guidelines for daily fiber intake, according to the Dietary Reference Intake (DRI), are as follows (Institute of Medicine (US) Panel on the Definition of Dietary Fibre and the Standing Committee on the Scientific Evaluation of Dietary Reference Intakes., 2001):

- "Children aged 1 to 3 years: 14 grams (g)
- Girls aged 4 to 8 years: 16.8 g
- Boys aged 4 to 8 years: 19.6 g
- Girls aged 9 to 13 years: 22.4 g
- Boys aged 9 to 13 years: 25.2 g
- Girls aged 14 to 18 years: 25.2 g
- Boys aged 14 to 18 years: 30.8 g
- Women aged 19 to 50 years: 25 g
- Men aged 19 to 50 years: 38 g
- Women aged 51 and older: 21 g
- Men aged 51 and older: 30 g"

Consuming more fiber has several positive effects on health, as stated in the above sections. Notably, the benefits of dietary fiber intake apply to both children and adults. To encourage higher fiber consumption from either food or supplements, it is crucial to improve communication and provide adequate education to consumers. When recommending daily dietary fiber intake, it is also important to consider that excessive consumption of dietary fiber can have detrimental effects, such as impaired iron absorption. While dietary fiber offers numerous health benefits, it's essential to strike a balance and not exceed the recommended intake to avoid potential complications.

6. Conclusions

Dietary fibers are the indigestible components of plant-based foods that pass through the digestive system relatively intact. Physicochemical characteristics of dietary fibers viz., solubility, viscosity and ability to undergo fermentation form the crux in determining its functionality within the gastrointestinal tract. These characteristics influence important factors like the availability of micronutrients, gut transit time, stool formation, and even the specificity of the gut microbiota. It not only supports healthy body weight management and metabolic function but also decreases cardiovascular disease risk and certain cancers and promotes overall colonic health. To obtain these health benefits, it is recommended to incorporate a diverse range of foods rich in fiber content into the daily diet. This includes vegetables, fruits, whole grains, pulses and nuts. By including these foods, individuals can ensure an adequate intake of dietary fiber and enhance their overall health and well-being.

Recent scientific studies have emphasized the significant role of dietary fiber in the prevention and management of various diseases, as well as its impact on mortality. The impact of different physicochemical characteristics of dietary fiber on its functionality should be explored in future research. By understanding these relationships more comprehensively, we can potentially maximize the effectiveness of specific types and doses of fiber in improving symptoms and outcomes in various disorders. This approach holds promise for achieving clinically meaningful improvements in the management of these conditions.

References

1. AACC (American Association of Cereal Chemists) (2001). The definition of dietary fiber. Report of the Dietary Fiber Definition Committee to the Board of Directors of the American Association of Cereal Chemists. *Cereal Foods World* , *46*(3), 112–126. URL <http://www.aaccnet.org/initiatives/definitions/Documents/Dietary Fiber/DFDef.pdf> Accessed 30.05.2023.
2. A.N.Z.F.A. (2001). Australia New Zealand Food Authority, Notice of a Proposed Change to Food Regulation and Further Invitation for Submissions. Application 277. *Inulin and Fructo-oligosaccharides as Dietary Fiber*, http://www.foodstandards.gov.au/srcfiles/A277 FA.pdf.
3. Aspinall, G. O. (1980). Chemistry of cell wall polysaccharides. In *Carbohydrates: Structure and function* (pp. 473-500). Academic Press.
4. Aune, D., Chan, D. S., Lau, R., Vieira, R., Greenwood, D. C., Kampman, E., & Norat, T. (2011). Dietary fibre, whole grains, and risk of colorectal cancer: systematic review and dose-response meta-analysis of prospective studies. *BMJ (Clinical research ed.), 343*, d6617. https://doi.org/10.1136/bmj.d6617
5. Barber, T. M., Kabisch, S., Pfeiffer, A. F. H., & Weickert, M. O. (2020). The Health Benefits of Dietary Fibre. *Nutrients, 12*(10), 3209. https://doi.org/10.3390/nu12103209

6. Ben, Q., Sun, Y., Chai, R., Qian, A., Xu, B., & Yuan, Y. (2014). Dietary fiber intake reduces risk for colorectal adenoma: a meta-analysis. *Gastroenterology,* *146*(3), 689–699.e6. https://doi.org/10.1053/j.gastro.2013.11.003
7. Biswas, V., Praveen, A., Marisetti, A. L., Sharma, A., Kumar, V., Sahu, S. K., & Tewari, D. (2022). A Mechanistic Overview on Impact of Dietary Fibres on Gut Microbiota and Its Association with Colon Cancer. *Dietetics, 1*(3), 182-202.
8. Brown, L., Rosner, B., Willett, W. W., & Sacks, F. M. (1999). Cholesterol-lowering effects of dietary fiber: a meta-analysis. *The American journal of clinical nutrition,* *69*(1), 30–42. https://doi.org/10.1093/ajcn/69.1.30
9. Burkitt D. (1991). An approach to the reduction of the most common Western cancers. The failure of therapy to reduce disease. *Archives of surgery (Chicago, Ill. : 1960),* *126*(3), 345–347. https://doi.org/10.1001/archsurg.1991.01410270089014
10. Burkitt D. P. (1971). Epidemiology of cancer of the colon and rectum. *Cancer,* *28(1),* 3–13. https://doi.org/10.1002/1097-0142(197107)28:1<3::aid-cncr2820280104>3.0.co;2-n
11. Burkitt D. P. (1973). Some diseases characteristic of modern Western civilization. *British medical journal,* *1*(5848), 274–278. https://doi.org/10.1136/bmj.1.5848.274
12. Chambers, E. S., Viardot, A., Psichas, A., Morrison, D. J., Murphy, K. G., Zac-Varghese, S. E., MacDougall,

K., Preston, T., Tedford, C., Finlayson, G. S., Blundell, J. E., Bell, J. D., Thomas, E. L., Mt-Isa, S., Ashby, D., Gibson, G. R., Kolida, S., Dhillo, W. S., Bloom, S. R., Morley, W., ... Frost, G. (2015). Effects of targeted delivery of propionate to the human colon on appetite regulation, body weight maintenance and adiposity in overweight adults. *Gut, 64*(11), 1744–1754. https://doi.org/10.1136/gutjnl-2014-307913

13. Chassaing, B., Koren, O., Goodrich, J. K., Poole, A. C., Srinivasan, S., Ley, R. E., & Gewirtz, A. T. (2015). Dietary emulsifiers impact the mouse gut microbiota promoting colitis and metabolic syndrome. *Nature, 519*(7541), 92–96. https://doi.org/10.1038/nature14232
14. Cronin, P., Joyce, S. A., O'Toole, P. W., & O'Connor, E. M. (2021). Dietary Fibre Modulates the Gut Microbiota. *Nutrients, 13*(5), 1655. https://doi.org/10.3390/nu13051655
15. Crowe, F. L., Appleby, P. N., Allen, N. E., & Key, T. J. (2011). Diet and risk of diverticular disease in Oxford cohort of European Prospective Investigation into Cancer and Nutrition (EPIC): prospective study of British vegetarians and non-vegetarians. *BMJ (Clinical research ed.), 343*, d4131. https://doi.org/10.1136/bmj.d4131
16. Cruz-Rubio, J. M., Loeppert, R., Viernstein, H., & Praznik, W. (2018). Trends in the use of plant non-starch polysaccharides within food, dietary supplements, and pharmaceuticals: beneficial effects on regulation and wellbeing of the intestinal tract. *Scientia Pharmaceutica, 86*(4), 49.

17. Cummings, J. H., Bingham, S. A., Heaton, K. W., & Eastwood, M. A. (1992). Fecal weight, colon cancer risk, and dietary intake of nonstarch polysaccharides (dietary fiber). *Gastroenterology, 103*(6), 1783-1789.
18. de Carvalho, C. M., de Paula, T. P., Viana, L. V., Machado, V. M., de Almeida, J. C., & Azevedo, M. J. (2017). Plasma glucose and insulin responses after consumption of breakfasts with different sources of soluble fiber in type 2 diabetes patients: a randomized crossover clinical trial. *The American journal of clinical nutrition, 106*(5), 1238–1245. https://doi.org/10.3945/ajcn.117.157263
19. Desai, M. S., Seekatz, A. M., Koropatkin, N. M., Kamada, N., Hickey, C. A., Wolter, M., Pudlo, N. A., Kitamoto, S., Terrapon, N., Muller, A., Young, V. B., Henrissat, B., Wilmes, P., Stappenbeck, T. S., Núñez, G., & Martens, E. C. (2016). A Dietary Fiber-Deprived Gut Microbiota Degrades the Colonic Mucus Barrier and Enhances Pathogen Susceptibility. *Cell, 167*(5), 1339–1353.e21. https://doi.org/10.1016/j.cell.2016.10.043
20. Dhingra, D., Michael, M., Rajput, H., & Patil, R. T. (2012). Dietary fibre in foods: a review. *Journal of food science and technology, 49*(3), 255–266. https://doi.org/10.1007/s13197-011-0365-5
21. Fuentes-Zaragoza, E., Riquelme-Navarrete, M. J., Sánchez-Zapata, E., & Pérez-Álvarez, J. A. (2010). Resistant starch as functional ingredient: A review. *Food Research International, 43*(4), 931-942.
22. Grooms, K. N., Ommerborn, M. J., Pham, D. Q., Djoussé, L., & Clark, C. R. (2013). Dietary fiber intake and cardiometabolic risks among US adults,

NHANES 1999-2010. *The American journal of medicine, 126*(12), 1059–67.e674. https://doi.org/10.1016/j.amjmed.2013.07.023

23. Hijová, E., Bertková, I., & Štofilová, J. (2019). Dietary fibre as prebiotics in nutrition. *Central European journal of public health*, 27(3), 251–255. https://doi.org/10.21101/cejph.a5313
24. Ho, Y. H., Tan, M., & Seow-Choen, F. (2000). Micronized purified flavonidic fraction compared favorably with rubber band ligation and fiber alone in the management of bleeding hemorrhoids: randomized controlled trial. *Diseases of the colon & rectum, 43*, 66-69.
25. Institute of Medicine (US) Panel on the Definition of Dietary Fiber and the Standing Committee on the Scientific Evaluation of Dietary Reference Intakes. (2001). Dietary Reference Intakes Proposed Definition of Dietary Fiber. National Academies Press (US), Soliman G. A. (2019). *Dietary Fiber, Atherosclerosis, and Cardiovascular Disease. Nutrients, 11*(5), 1155. https://doi.org/10.3390/nu11051155
26. Jenkins, D. J., Leeds, A. R., Gassull, M. A., Cochet, B., & Alberti, G. M. (1977). Decrease in postprandial insulin and glucose concentrations by guar and pectin. *Annals of internal medicine, 86*(1), 20–23. https://doi.org/10.7326/0003-4819-86-1-20
27. Kay R. M. (1982). Dietary fiber. Journal of lipid research, 23(2), 221–242.
28. Khalid, W., Arshad, M. S., Jabeen, A., Muhammad Anjum, F., Qaisrani, T. B., & Suleria, H. A. R. (2022). Fiber-enriched botanicals: A therapeutic tool against

certain metabolic ailments. *Food Science & Nutrition, 10*(10), 3203-3218.

29. Lara-Espinoza, C., Carvajal-Millán, E., Balandrán-Quintana, R., López-Franco, Y., & Rascón-Chu, A. (2018). Pectin and Pectin-Based Composite Materials: Beyond Food Texture. Molecules (Basel, Switzerland), 23(4), 942. https://doi.org/10.3390/molecules23040942
30. Li, Z., Yi, C. X., Katiraei, S., Kooijman, S., Zhou, E., Chung, C. K., Gao, Y., van den Heuvel, J. K., Meijer, O. C., Berbée, J. F. P., Heijink, M., Giera, M., Willems van Dijk, K., Groen, A. K., Rensen, P. C. N., & Wang, Y. (2018). Butyrate reduces appetite and activates brown adipose tissue via the gut-brain neural circuit. *Gut, 67*(7), 1269–1279. https://doi.org/10.1136/gutjnl-2017-314050
31. Mao, T., Huang, F., Zhu, X., Wei, D., & Chen, L. (2021). Effects of dietary fiber on glycemic control and insulin sensitivity in patients with type 2 diabetes: A systematic review and meta-analysis. *Journal of Functional Foods, 82*, 104500.
32. Millar, S. R., Navarro, P., Harrington, J. M., Shivappa, N., Hébert, J. R., Perry, I. J., & Phillips, C. M. (2021). Comparing dietary score associations with lipoprotein particle subclass profiles: A cross-sectional analysis of a middle-to older-aged population. *Clinical nutrition (Edinburgh, Scotland), 40*(7), 4720–4729. https://doi.org/10.1016/j.clnu.2021.06.005
33. Mudgil, D. (2017). The interaction between insoluble and soluble fiber. In *Dietary fiber for the prevention of cardiovascular disease* (pp. 35-59). Academic Press.

34. Müller-Lissner, S. A., Kamm, M. A., Scarpignato, C., & Wald, A. (2005). Myths and misconceptions about chronic constipation. *Official journal of the American College of Gastroenterology| ACG, 100*(1), 232-242.
35. Murphy, N., Norat, T., Ferrari, P., Jenab, M., Bueno-de-Mesquita, B., Skeie, G., Dahm, C. C., Overvad, K., Olsen, A., Tjønneland, A., Clavel-Chapelon, F., Boutron-Ruault, M. C., Racine, A., Kaaks, R., Teucher, B., Boeing, H., Bergmann, M. M., Trichopoulou, A., Trichopoulos, D., Lagiou, P., ... Riboli, E. (2012). Dietary fibre intake and risks of cancers of the colon and rectum in the European prospective investigation into cancer and nutrition (EPIC). *PloS one, 7*(6), e39361. https://doi.org/10.1371/journal.pone.0039361
36. Opoku-Acheampong, I., McLaud, T., & Anderson, O. S. (2022). Fecal Microbiota Transplantation to Prevent and Treat Chronic Disease: Implications for Dietetics Practice. *Journal of the Academy of Nutrition and Dietetics, 122*(1), 33–37. https://doi.org/10.1016/j.jand.2021.08.112
37. Parikh, S., Pollock, N. K., Bhagatwala, J., Guo, D. H., Gutin, B., Zhu, H., & Dong, Y. (2012). Adolescent fiber consumption is associated with visceral fat and inflammatory markers. *The Journal of clinical endocrinology and metabolism, 97*(8), E1451–E1457. https://doi.org/10.1210/jc.2012-1784
38. Park, Y., Subar, A. F., Hollenbeck, A., & Schatzkin, A. (2011). Dietary fiber intake and mortality in the NIH-AARP diet and health study. *Archives of internal medicine, 171*(12), 1061–1068. https://doi.org/10.1001/archinternmed.2011.18

39. Queiroz-Monici, K. D. S., Costa, G. E., da Silva, N., Reis, S. M., & de Oliveira, A. C. (2005). Bifidogenic effect of dietary fiber and resistant starch from leguminous on the intestinal microbiota of rats. *Nutrition, 21*(5), 602-608.
40. Reynolds, A. N., Akerman, A., Kumar, S., Diep Pham, H. T., Coffey, S., & Mann, J. (2022). Dietary fibre in hypertension and cardiovascular disease management: systematic review and meta-analyses. *BMC medicine, 20*(1), 139.
41. Slavin J. L. (1987). Dietary fiber: classification, chemical analyses, and food sources. *Journal of the American Dietetic Association, 87*(9), 1164–1171.
42. Tang, M., Li, S., Wei, L., Hou, Z., Qu, J., & Li, L. (2021). Do engineered nanomaterials affect immune responses by interacting with gut microbiota?. *Frontiers in Immunology, 12*, 684605.
43. Theander, O., Aman, P. (1979). The chemistry, morphology and analysis of dietary fibre component. In: Inglett G, Falkehag, editors. *Dietary fibres: chemistry and nutrition* (pp. 214–244). New York: Academic.
44. Tong, L. T., Zhong, K., Liu, L., Qiu, J., Guo, L., Zhou, X., Cao, L., & Zhou, S. (2014). Effects of dietary wheat bran arabinoxylans on cholesterol metabolism of hypercholesterolemic hamsters. *Carbohydrate polymers, 112*, 1–5. https://doi.org/10.1016/j.carbpol.2014.05.061
45. Trumbo, P., Schlicker, S., Yates, A. A., & Poos, M. (2002). Dietary reference intakes for energy, carbohydrate, fiber, fat, fatty acids, cholesterol,

protein and amino acids.(Commentary). *Journal of the american dietetic association, 102*(11), 1621-1631.

46. Tungland, B. C., & Meyer, D. (2002). Nondigestible oligo-and polysaccharides (Dietary Fiber): their physiology and role in human health and food. *Comprehensive reviews in food science and food safety, 1*(3), 90-109.
47. Van Denffer, D., Schumacher, W., Magdefrau, K., Ehrendorfer, F. (1976). Excretory and secretory tissues. In: *Strasbueger's textbook of botany* (pp 118–121). Longman, New York.
48. Vijay, A., & Valdes, A. M. (2022). Role of the gut microbiome in chronic diseases: a narrative review. *European journal of clinical nutrition, 76*(4), 489–501. https://doi.org/10.1038/s41430-021-00991-6
49. Weickert, M. O., & Pfeiffer, A. F. (2008). Metabolic effects of dietary fiber consumption and prevention of diabetes. *The Journal of nutrition, 138*(3), 439–442. https://doi.org/10.1093/jn/138.3.439

3.

BOOSTING NUTRITIONAL VALUE: THE IMPORTANCE OF FOOD FORTIFICATION

Sonia*, Neha, Bhavna and Raveena

Department of Foods and Nutrition, CCS HAU, Hisar, Haryana- 125004

Email: sonia08hau@gmail.com

Abstract

It is widely acknowledged that hidden hunger is a significant public health issue in low- and middle-income nations (LMIC) that severely impedes national development and sustained economic progress. The fortification of food mediums with micronutrients is becoming an attractive and long-lasting alternative to intravenous and oral supplementation. In Switzerland, table salt iodization was first implemented as a public health intervention in the early 1920s to prevent endemic goiter. Numerous researches have been done which demonstrating how effective fortification is by using different vehicles. During the 1920s and 1930s, the U.S. began iodizing salt and fortifying margarine with vitamin-A, flour and bread were enriched with mineral iron and B-complex in the 1940s. Consequently, many diseases caused by vitamin and mineral deficiencies, such as night blindness, goiter, rickets, beriberi, and pellagra, have essentially disappeared as a result of these efforts. The use of flour enhanced with folate has been linked to large declines in folate-related NTDs in North America. Iodized salt was made mandatory in over 130 nations, cereal grain (wheat, rice, or maize) fortification was mandated in 80 nations, and milk and edible oils are being fortified in numerous more nations. The practice of mandating vitamin-A addition to Vanaspati dates back to the 1950s and is still experienced today in India. The application of the salt iodization plan in India has been a huge public health achievement, and it provides significant insights and inspires confidence in the fortification of common foods to eradicate micronutrients deficiencies in our population. Food fortification is a globally applicable, scientifically validated, affordable, sustainable and scalable solution that tackles the problem of vitamin and mineral deficiencies.

Keywords: Deficiency, Fortification, Micronutrients, Supplementation, Sustainable

1. Introduction to "food fortification"

This chapter provides an overview of food fortification, its purpose in addressing nutrient deficiencies, the historical background of fortification efforts, the significance of fortification in public health, an understanding of micronutrients and their importance in human health, highlights common micronutrient deficiencies worldwide, explores the health implications and the consequences of these deficiencies, and identifies the target populations for food fortification interventions.

2. Definition and purpose of food fortification

Fortification refers to "the practice of deliberately increasing the content of an essential micronutrient, i.e.

vitamins and minerals (including trace elements) such as Iron, Iodine, Zinc, Vitamins A & D to staple foods such as rice, wheat, oil, milk and salt to improve their nutritional content to improve the nutritional quality of the food supply and to provide a public health benefit with minimal risk to health" **(WHO & FAO).** Food fortification is used to address a number of issues and prevent nutrient deficiencies in populations, improve public health, and promote overall well-being. It is a practical way to increase the nutrient content of commonly consumed foods and ensure adequate intake of key vitamins, minerals, and other vital micronutrients.

3. Historical background and importance of food fortification

Iodine was initially added to salt in the early 20th century to prevent goitre, beginning the method of food fortification. Fortification programmes have grown over time to incorporate more necessary minerals like iron, vitamin A, folate, and zinc. Fortification efforts have evolved globally, with the establishment of national programs, international guidelines, and collaboration between governments, NGOs, and the business sector. Vitamin and Mineral deficiencies, also known as hidden hunger, pose significant health risks, particularly in vulnerable populations. Lack of essential nutrients can lead to various health problems, impaired cognitive development, weakened immune systems, and increased susceptibility to diseases. Food fortification serves as an effective means to address these deficiencies on a large scale, reaching diverse populations with minimal behaviour change or disruption to existing dietary habits.

4. Overview of micronutrients and their common deficiencies

Micronutrients are vital vitamins and minerals that the body needs in tiny amounts for optimum health and performance. They are essential to many physiological functions including energy-metabolism, growth and development, immune function, bone health, and cognitive function (FAO/WHO, 2004). The key micronutrients include iron, zinc, iodine, calcium, vitamin-A, vitamin-D, vitamin-B12 and folate. Micronutrient malnutrition is the lack of certain micronutrients. Its impacts include nutrient-deficit disorders, weakened immune systems, higher baby and maternal death rates, mental and physical impairment in children, and a host of other problems. Particularly during the first 1,000 days of a kid's existence, child health and survival are negatively impacted. Serious cognitive and bodily effects may follow from this. A person's health and well-being can be negatively impacted by even mild to moderate deficits, which can also impede socioeconomic advancement. A deficiency in vitamins and minerals is referred to as "hidden hunger" by the World Health Organisation. This happens when the calibre of the food consumed falls short of nutrient requirements. Micronutrients, such as the vitamins and minerals required for growth and development, are therefore lacking in the diet. Essential vitamin and mineral deficiencies (sometimes known as "hidden hunger" or "micronutrient deficiencies") are serious public health issues in many parts of the world, especially among the people of low- and middle-income countries (LMIC).

- It has been calculated that MNDs make up 7.3 per cent of the worldwide illness burden overall, and that iron and vitamin A deficiency are two of the top 15 factors that contribute to the deaths of almost a million children each year.
- According to WHO estimates, 37 per cent of pregnant women and 40 per cent of children under the age of five are anaemic worldwide (WHO Anaemia; 2023); for their offspring, vitamin deficiencies in utero can result in low birth weight and brain and spinal abnormalities.
- In 2020, the prevalence of overweight in children under 5 was projected to be 5.7 per cent or 38.9 million worldwide.
- An estimated 6.7 per cent of children under the age of five worldwide, or 45.4 million, were still in danger of dying from wasting in 2020.
- Around the world, stunting afflicted 149.2 million children under the age of five in 2020, or an estimated 22.0 per cent.

Additionally, India has a very high prevalence of micronutrient deficiencies brought on by low levels of vitamin A, iodine, iron, and folic acid, which can result in anaemia, goitres, night blindness, and other birth defects. According to a few state-wide surveys, the National Nutrition Monitoring Bureau (NNMB) of the National Institute of Nutrition (NIN), Government of India, found that between 50% and 94% of people in various states across India experience vitamin-D deficiency. Nearly 62% of the Indian population has low serum blood levels of vitamin-A. Micronutrient deficiencies result in negative functional consequences such as stunted growth, greater vulnerability to infections, physical impairments, cognitive deficits, blindness, and early mortality.

According to the National Family Health Survey (NFHS-4; 2015-16)

- **35.7 per cent** Children under 5 years of age are underweight,
- **58.4 per cent** Children (6-59 months) are suffering from anemia
- **22.7 per cent** Men are suffering from anemia
- Anaemia affects **53.1 per cent** women of reproductive age.

The most typical nutritional deficiencies are iron, zinc, iodine, and vitamin A. (Diaz *et al.*, 2003). Some of the most prevalent deficiencies include-

4.1. Vitamin-A deficiency (VAD)

The deficiency of Vitamin-A is a widespread problem, particularly developing countries. It affects the vision, body's system of defence, overall development and growth of teenagers and an increased risk of infectious diseases like diarrhoea and measles. The most common preventable cause of childhood blindness is VAD (WHO, 2019).

4.2. Iron deficiency

One of the most common micronutrient deficits that affect both industrialised and developing nations is iron insufficiency. It may result in iron-deficiency anaemia, which is marked by weakness and exhaustion, impaired cognitive function, reduced work productivity and compromised immune function. (Stoltzfus, 2003).

4.3. Iodine deficiency

It is a significant public-health issue, primarily affecting individuals in mountainous and landlocked areas where iodine-rich foods or iodized salt are not widely available. It can result in goiter, a visible enlargement of the thyroid gland. In severe cases, it can lead to intellectual and developmental disabilities, particularly in children. Iodine-deficient pregnant women are more likely to experience pregnancy difficulties and may give birth to children who have cognitive impairment.

4.4. Zinc deficiency

Zinc deficiency is prevalent in many developing countries, especially amongst susceptible populations such as pregnant women and children. It can impact growth, immune function, and cognitive development. Pregnant women with zinc deficiency may experience adverse birth outcomes. Zinc deficiency increases the risk of infectious diseases and is associated with stunting, delayed sexual maturation, and impaired neuro-development in children. (Wessells & Brown, 2012)

5. Target populations for food fortification

Certain population groups are particularly vulnerable to micronutrient deficiencies and are considered priority targets for food fortification programs. Food fortification strategies aim to reach these populations and ensure their adequate intake of essential micronutrients to mitigate the health risks associated with deficiencies. These populations may include:

5.1. Women of reproductive age

Women, especially when lactating and pregnant, have increased nutrient requirements. Fortifying foods targeted at this population group can help prevent deficiencies in key nutrients such as folate and iron, which are critical for maternal and child health (Shulkin *et al.*, 2018).

5.2. Infants and young children

The formative years of childhood are crucial for growth and development, making infants and young children susceptible to micronutrient deficiencies. Fortifying complementary foods, such as infant cereals and fortified baby formulas, can help address nutrient gaps during this vulnerable stage (Neufeld *et al.*, 2017).

5.3. School-age children

Due to their growth and physical activity, school-age children frequently have significant nutrient needs. Fortifying staple foods commonly consumed by this population group, such as fortified rice or wheat flour, can ensure the availability of essential nutrients for their overall health and cognitive development (Suchdev *et al.*, 2020).

5.4. Marginalized and low-income populations

Socioeconomically disadvantaged populations, including those living in poverty or in distant parts with limited access to diverse and nutritious foods are more prone to nutrient deficiencies. Targeting fortification interventions toward these populations can help alleviate disparities in nutrient intake and improve health outcomes (Mason *et al.*, 2014).

6. Food fortification of staples

6.1. Fortification of cereals and cereal products

Fortification of staple foods, such as cereal and cereal products, is a widely recognized strategy for addressing nutrient deficiencies and improving public health. By adding essential micronutrients to these commonly consumed foods, fortification programs aim to enhance the nutritional status of populations, particularly in regions where access to a diverse diet is limited. Cereal and cereal products, including wheat, wheat-flour, rice, and maize, are ideal vehicles for fortification due to their widespread consumption and high nutritional value. Flour, biscuits and breads, being commonly consumed food items; serve as ideal vehicles for fortification. The addition of essential micronutrients, such as folic acid, iron, and B-complex vitamins, can enhance the overall nutritional profile of these foods and successfully address nutrient deficits.

Impact and benefits of cereal fortification

Cereal fortification has demonstrated numerous benefits in improving public health and reducing the prevalence of nutrient deficiencies. Studies have shown that fortification programs can effectively increase micronutrient intake and address specific deficiencies. For instance, iron-fortified cereals (wheat and rice) have been successful in lowering the prevalence of anaemia caused by a lack of iron, particularly in vulnerable populations like children and women of reproductive age (Zimmermann *et al.*, 2010 and Vist *et al.*, 2011). The prevalence of neural tube abnormalities has been successfully decreased by fortifying flour with folic acid. (Crider *et al.*, 2011).

Fortified cereals offer a practical and cost-effective approach to reach large populations, including susceptible populations like children and expectant mothers. Additionally, fortification can contribute to increased productivity and improved cognitive development, resulting in enhanced economic outcomes at both individual and societal levels (Horton *et al.*, 2006).

6.2. Fortification of edible oils

Edible oil fortification involves the addition of essential vitamins, such as vitamins A and D, to commonly consumed oils. This fortification strategy aims to combat vitamin deficiencies and improve overall nutritional status. The proper selection of fortificants and adequate quality control measures are crucial to maintain the stability and bio-availability of added vitamins during oil processing, storage, and cooking. Edible oil fortification has shown promising results in addressing vitamin A deficiency and reducing associated health risks (Sommer & West, 1996).

Impact and benefits of edible oil fortification

Edible oil fortification has been related with improved vitamin-A status, reduced morbidity and mortality rates, and enhanced immune function (Handu *et al.*, 2021).

6.3. Fortification of milk and milk products

The fortification of milk and milk products is an important strategy to enhance their nutritional value and address nutrient deficiencies in populations, particularly in regions where dairy consumption is widespread. Milk and milk products are rich sources of essential nutrients such as calcium, vitamin-D, vitamin-B12, and protein. Fortifying these products can further enhance their nutritional composition and contribute to meeting recommended dietary intakes. Common fortificants include vitamin-D, iron, omega-3 fatty acids, and pro-biotics, which can be added to milk or incorporated into dairy-based products such as yogurt and cheese.

Impact and benefits of milk and milk product fortification

The fortification of milk and milk products has the potential to improve the nutritional status and health outcomes of populations, particularly in vulnerable group such as children, pregnant women, and the elderly. Yogurt and fermented milk products are known for their pro-biotic content and unique sensory characteristics. Fortifying these products can further enhance their nutritional composition and contribute to improved health outcomes. Common fortificants include vitamins, minerals, pre-biotics, and pro-biotics, which can be added during the production process to increase the nutrient content and functionality of products. For example, vitamin D-fortified milk has been successful in improving vitamin D status and reducing the risk of deficiency-related diseases (Smith *et al.*, 2017). Regular consumption of fortified dairy products has been associated with improved bone health, reduced the risk of osteoporosis, enhanced cognitive function, and improved gut health. Fortification can further enhance the nutritional quality of dairy products, contributing to these positive health outcomes (Weaver & Plawecki, 1994). Fortification of yogurt and fermented milk products has the potential to improve the nutritional status and gut health of consumers. Research has shown that fortification can effectively increase the intake of targeted nutrients and enhance the probiotic content, resulting in improved digestion, immune function, and overall well-being. For example, vitamin D-fortified yogurt has been successful in improving vitamin D status and promoting bone health (Holick & Chen, 2008).

6.4. Fortification of table salt and salt substitutes

Fortification of table salt is a widely practiced strategy to address nutrient deficiencies and improve public health outcomes. This intervention primarily aims to address iodine deficiency disorders (IDD), iron deficiency anemia, and dental fluorosis. Salt iodization is a successful public health intervention aimed at preventing iodine deficiency disorders (IDD), such as goiter and mental impairment. Salt fortification involves the addition of essential micronutrients, such as iodine, iron, and fluoride, to table salt. Salt iodization programs have been implemented globally, contributing to significant improvements in population iodine status and the reduction of IDD (Andersson *et al.*, 2012). The fortification process must ensure that the added nutrients are stable and bio-available, while maintaining the sensory properties of salt.

Double fortified salt

Double fortified salt is an innovative approach that combines the fortification of salt with multiple nutrients. Typically, iron and iodine are added to table salt to address both iron and iodine deficiencies. Double fortified salt has been successfully used in regions where deficiencies in both micronutrients are common. This approach helps to overcome the challenges of implementing separate fortification programs and promotes the consumption of a single fortified product.

Impact and benefits of salt fortification

The fortification of table salt has had significant impacts on public health. Salt iodization programs have effectively reduced iodine deficiencies and related health problems, such as goiter and cognitive impairments (MB, 2009). Double fortified salt can simultaneously address iron and iodine deficiencies, which are common in many populations, leading to improved nutritional status and reduced anemia rates (Hess *et al.*, 2010). Evidence suggests that salt iodization programs have effectively reduced the prevalence of iodine deficiency disorders and improved cognitive function, particularly in children (Bleichrodt & Born, 1994).

7. Successful Indian national fortification programs

India has made significant progress in addressing micronutrient deficiencies through national fortification programs. This highlights successful fortification initiatives in India and discusses their impact on public health.

7.1. National Iodine Deficiency Disorders Control Program (NIDDCP, 1992)

NIDDCP in India aims to combat iodine deficiency and prevent iodine deficiency disorders (IDD). Through the mandatory iodization of salt, this program has been successful in eliminating deficiency of iodine as a public health problem. The salt iodization has achieved significant coverage, and regular monitoring ensures the sustainability and effectiveness of the program (Pandav *et al.*, 2013).

7.2. National Iron Plus Initiative (NIPI, 2013)

The Ministry of Family and Health Welfare in 2013 launched NIPI as a comprehensive program that addresses iron-deficiency anemia, particularly among susceptible populations such as pregnant women and children. It includes multiple strategies, including iron-folic acid supplementation, dietary diversification, and the fortification of staple foods. The fortification of wheat flour with iron has shown promising results in reducing anemia prevalence among targeted groups (Haas *et al.*, 2014).

7.3. National Vitamin A Prophylaxis Program (NVAPP, 1970)

This aims to prevent deficiency of vitamin-A and its associated health consequences. Under this, children between the ages of 6 months and 5 years old are given high-dose vitamin A supplements every two years. This program has been successful in reducing the prevalence of vitamin-A deficiency and improving child survival rates (Singh & West, 2004).

7.4. Milk Fortification

India has also implemented milk fortification programs to address the micronutrient deficiencies. The fortification of milk with essential minerals and vitamins, such as vitamin-A and -D, has been successfully scaled up in various states. These programs have significantly contributed to improving the nutritional quality of milk consumed by the population (Eichler *et al.*, 2012).

7.5. Integrated Child Development Services Scheme (ICDS, 1975)

The Government of India's flagship programme, ICDS, focuses on the overall development of mothers and children under the age of six. As part of the scheme, the fortification of take-home rations provided to the children and pregnant women with essential nutrients has been implemented. This intervention has improved the nutrient intake and nutritional status of the target population (MWCD, 2023).

8. Conclusions

Fortification of staple foods is a viable method for enhancing population health and nutritional status, particularly in areas with limited dietary diversity. The systematic addition of essential micronutrients to these staple foods has demonstrated significant impact and cost-effectiveness. By adding essential micronutrients to these widely consumed grains, fortification programs can effectively address nutrient deficiencies and improve public health. The efficacy and long-term viability of fortification programmes, however, depend on constant monitoring, assessment, and stakeholder participation in order to overcome implementation obstacles. Ensuring safety, quality, and regulatory compliance of fortified foods is crucial for the success and effectiveness of food fortification programs. Countries can overcome obstacles and guarantee the effective execution of food fortification programmes to enhance public health and treat nutrient shortages by recognising and proactively addressing the issues. By adopting a strong regulatory approach, countries can successfully implement and sustain food fortification programs to address nutrient deficiencies and improve public health outcomes.

References

1. Andersson, M., Karumbunathan, V., & Zimmermann, M. B. (2012). Global iodine status in 2011 and trends over the past decade. *The Journal of nutrition*, *142*(4), 744-750.
2. WHO Anemia; 2023, https://www.who.int/news-room/fact-sheets/detail/anaemia.
3. Bleichrodt, N. & Born, M. P. (1994). "Meta-Analysis of Research on Iodine and Its Relationship to Cognitive Development" In: J. B. Stanbury, Ed., The Damaged Brain of Iodine Deficiency, Cognizant Communication Corporation, New York, pp. 195-200.
4. Crider, K. S., Bailey, L. B., & Berry, R. J. (2011). Folic acid food fortification—its history, effect, concerns, and future directions. *Nutrients*, *3*(3), 370-384.
5. Diaz, J. R., De Las Cagigas, A., & Rodriguez, R. (2003). Micronutrient deficiencies in developing and affluent countries. *European journal of clinical nutrition*, *57*(1), S70-S72.
6. Eichler, K., Wieser, S., Rüthemann, I., & Brügger, U. (2012). Effects of micronutrient fortified milk and cereal food for infants and children: a systematic review. *Bmc public health*, *12*, 1-13.
7. Haas, J. D., Rahn, M., Venkatramanan, S., Marquis, G. S., Wenger, M. J., Murray-Kolb, L. E., ... & Reinhart, G. A. (2014). Double-fortified salt is efficacious in improving indicators of iron deficiency in female

Indian tea pickers. *The Journal of nutrition*, *144*(6), 957-964.

8. Handu, S., Jan, S., Chauhan, K., & Saxena, D. C. (2021). Vitamin D fortification: A perspective to improve immunity for COVID-19 infection. *Functional Food Science*, *1*(10), 50-66.
9. Hess, S. Y. (2010). The impact of common micronutrient deficiencies on iodine and thyroid metabolism: the evidence from human studies. *Best Practice & Research Clinical Endocrinology & Metabolism*, *24*(1), 117-132.
10. Holick, M. F., & Chen, T. C. (2008). Vitamin D deficiency: a worldwide problem with health consequences. *The American journal of clinical nutrition*, *87*(4), 1080S-1086S.
11. Horton, S., 2006. The economics of food fortification. Journal of Nutrition, 136, 1068- 1071.
12. Mason, J. B., Shrimpton, R., Saldanha, L. S., Ramakrishnan, U., Victora, C. G., Girard, A. W., ... & Martorell, R. (2014). The first 500 days of life: policies to support maternal nutrition. *Global health action*, *7*(1), 23623.
13. MB, Z. (2009). Iodine deficiency. *Endocr Rev*, *30*, 376-408.
14. Ministry of Women and Child Development. Integrated Child Development Services (ICDS) Scheme. Government of India. http://icds-wcd.nic.in/icds.aspx.
15. Neufeld, L. M., Baker, S., Garrett, G. S., & Haddad, L. (2017). Coverage and utilization in food fortification programs: critical and neglected areas of

evaluation. *The Journal of nutrition*, *147*(5), 1015S-1019S.
16. NFHS-4th http://rchiips.org/nfhs/nfhs-4Reports/India.pdf.
17. Pandav, C. S., Yadav, K., Srivastava, R., Pandav, R., & Karmarkar, M. G. (2013). Iodine deficiency disorders (IDD) control in India. *The Indian journal of medical research*, *138*(3), 418.
18. Shulkin, M., Pimpin, L., Bellinger, D., Kranz, S., Fawzi, W., Duggan, C., & Mozaffarian, D. (2018). n–3 Fatty acid supplementation in mothers, preterm infants, and term infants and childhood psychomotor and visual development: a systematic review and meta-analysis. *The Journal of nutrition*, *148*(3), 409-418.
19. Singh, V., & West, K. P. (2004). Vitamin A deficiency and xerophthalmia among school-aged children in Southeastern Asia. *European journal of clinical nutrition*, *58*(10), 1342-1349.
20. Smith, L. M., Gallagher, J. C., & Suiter, C. (2017). Medium doses of daily vitamin D decrease falls and higher doses of daily vitamin D3 increase falls: a randomized clinical trial. *The Journal of steroid biochemistry and molecular biology*, *173*, 317-322.
21. Sommer, A., & West, K. P. (1996). *Vitamin A deficiency: health, survival, and vision.* Oxford University Press, USA.
22. Stoltzfus, R. J. (2003). Iron deficiency: global prevalence and consequences. *Food and nutrition bulletin*, *24*(4_suppl_1), S99-S103.
23. Suchdev, P. S., Jefferds, M. E. D., Ota, E., da Silva Lopes, K., & De-Regil, L. M. (2020). Home

fortification of foods with multiple micronutrient powders for health and nutrition in children under two years of age. *Cochrane database of systematic reviews*, (2).

24. Vist, G. E., Suchdev, P. S., De-Regil, L. M., Walleser, S., & Peña-Rosas, J. P. (2011). Home fortification of foods with multiple micronutrient powders for health and nutrition in children under 2 years of age. *Cochrane Database of Systematic Reviews*, (1).
25. Weaver, C. M., & Plawecki, K. L. (1994). Dietary calcium: adequacy of a vegetarian diet. *The American journal of clinical nutrition*, *59*(5), 1238S-1241S.
26. Wessells, K. R., & Brown, K. H. (2012). Estimating the global prevalence of zinc deficiency: results based on zinc availability in national food supplies and the prevalence of stunting. *PloS one*, *7*(11), e50568.
27. World Health Organization. (2009). Global prevalence of vitamin A deficiency in populations at risk 1995-2005: WHO global database on vitamin A deficiency. https://www.who.int/publications/i/item/9789241598019.
28. Zimmermann, M. B., Chassard, C., Rohner, F., N'goran, E. K., Nindjin, C., Dostal, A., ... & Hurrell, R. F. (2010). The effects of iron fortification on the gut microbiota in African children: a randomized controlled trial in Cote d'Ivoire. *The American journal of clinical nutrition*, *92*(6), 1406-1415.

4.

CONSUMER PROBLEMS AND PROTECTION IN INDIA: ADULTERATION, COUNTERFEIT PRODUCTS, BLACK MARKETING AND HOARDING

Rupanagudi Unesha Fareq, PhD Scholar, Department of Family Resource Management, College of Home Science, GB Pant University of Agriculture and Technology, Pantnagar, Uttarakhand.

Rupanagudi Beena Fareq, PhD Scholar, Department of Apparel and Textile Sciences, College of Community Science, University of Agricultural Sciences, Dharwad, Karnataka

Email: unirupanagudi@gmail.com

Abstract

Every person utilises the a range of daily purchases of goods and services. Whatever they buy, consume, and use must be paid for in order for them to feel satisfied. They aren't always happy with the items they buy, though. Anyone who purchases or utilises products or services is a consumer. Goods include both durable products like televisions, refrigerators, and bicycles as well as consumables like flour, pulses, salt, sugar, fruit etc. Services include things like transportation, electricity, telephone, and movie screenings. Usually, when someone uses products and services, that person is referred to as a "consumer." Consumers may be tricked by dishonest businesspeople, including traders, dealers, producers, and manufacturers as well as service providers, in a numerous methods. One must have considered about the following unethical actions at some point: (i) Adulteration is the practise of tainting a product being offered with something subpar. (ii) The sale of fake goods, often known as counterfeit goods, refers to the act of selling something worthless in place of an authentic good. (iii) Hoarding and black marketing is the practise of buying necessities in large quantities and reselling them at sky-high rates on the black market when commodities are in high demand. Protecting customers' interests and rights is part of consumer protection. In other terms, it refers to the actions taken to safeguard customers from dishonest and unethical company practises and to quickly resolve their complaints.

Keywords: Consumer problems, Consumer Protection, Adulteration, counterfeit products, hoarding ,blackmarketing

1. Introduction

India has a substantial population, creating significant opportunities in every industry related to manufacturing and marketing. Every firm is trying to maximise profits in India's contemporary environment of intense competition and globalisation while using such destructive and dishonest promotion , marketing techniques, disregarding the comforts of consumers. In order to safeguard their own interests, Consumers/buyers must be well-informed about the products or services they are using (Chatar and Sanjay, 2020).

Every person utilises the daily purchases of a range of products and services. They must pay for everything they purchase, consume, and enjoy using. They aren't always happy with the items they purchase, though. Anyone who purchases goods or services from seller is referred to as a consumer. Consumable commodities like flour, sugar, fruit etc. are considered goods, as are long-lasting items like bicycles, refrigerators, and televisions. Electricity, transportation, movies, and other services are examples of services. All customers are defrauded in some form or another, which is bad for everyone's health since we are all consumers.

A "consumer" is a term used to describe someone who uses or consumes products and services. Following the LPG policy of 1991, consumerism became more and more popular in India. As a result, consumers are now readily taken advantage of in the market through adulteration, fraudulent items, black marketing and hoarding, the use of erroneous measures and weights, deceptive advertising, and other tactics. Indian consumers are frequently taken advantage of in the market because they are unaware of their rights. Consumers have the freedom to accept or reject products without disturbing about being taken benefit of (Manoj, 2020).

Consumers must be conscious of their rights and responsibilities, confirm the suggested Market retail price (MRP) of products, study the legal papers before signing them, and exercise extreme attention when making big purchases like real estate. There is a chance of food poisoning at the very least, so it is very necessary to verify the manufacturing and expiry date, ingredients list, and other information before buying consumer durables like food, groceries, and other items. The India's Consumer Protection Act of 1986, which includes various measures of protection in both the purchase of goods and the providing of services, marked the beginning of the consumer protection movement in contemporary India. Both consumers and the government must take aggressive steps to defend one another's interests as consumers(Aggarwal, 2021; Ganesan and Sumathy, 2012).

2. Objective

To gain insight on food adulteration, counterfeit products, black marketing and hoarding and legal ways of protection in India

The modern era is acknowledged as the "consumer era." No country may, whether intentionally or unintentionally, disregard consumer concerns. On the basis of the speedy enactment of consumer protection laws in practically every region of the world, this can be stated (Sahoo and Chatterjee, 2009). In order to guarantee that people uphold their rights as consumers, the Consumer Protection Act creates stronger regulations for consumer issues. Consumer exploitation has been recommended with harsh punishments. The government's decision to prioritise consumer protection is consistent with its commitment to transforming India into a prosperous market for consumers in the future. The consumer must be knowledgeable about his rights and take an active part. The government has made numerous constitutional measures to safeguard consumers.

3. Consumer protection act

CPA is applicable to all products, services, and unfair trade practices and to all industries, whether they are private, public, or cooperative, unless officially relieved by the central government. In order to advance and defend consumer rights, it established consumer protection councils at the national, state, district levels. It also creates a three-tiered quasi-judicial system to resolve consumer complaints and disputes.

National, State and District Commissions are authorized to hear complaints in cases where the price of the goods or services received in exchange for payment does not exceed 2 crore rupees for national level ,exceed 50 lakh rupees but not more than 2 crores for state level and does not exceed 50 lakhs for district level .

The Consumer Protection Act of 2019 mandates that every complaint be resolved as quickly as possible, and that every effort must be made to reach a decision on the complaint within 3 months of the date the opposing party receives notice, or within 5 months if the complaint calls for the analysis or testing of goods.

4. Consumer problems

4.1. Food adulteration

The addition of something inferior to the offered product is known as adulteration. Food is regularly contaminated so as to feed the big population as well as this expanding population (Hamburg, 2010). Food adulteration typically takes the simplest possible form, with illegal drugs being partially or completely substituted. Various factors, such as monetary gain, negligence, and improper hygienicand handling conditions during manufacturing,processing, storing, transporting, and selling, can lead to food adulteration. As a result, consumers who consume contaminated goods are either deceived or become sick as a result (Abhirami and Radha, 2015).

These days, it is challenging to locate a segment of the food market that is unadulterated. The large volume of imported food and the rising amount of food producers, it is crucial for consumers to understand adulterants and impact on health. Otherwise, producers may deceive and scam consumers.

Chemicals known as adulterants, which are substances that shouldn't be in food or drink, might be purposefully added to food substances to increase their apparent quantities, lower their manufacturing costs, or for some unlawful reason (Anita and Neetu, 2013 and Choudary, 2020).

Food items and drinks are typically contaminated for the six reasons listed below (Narayan,2014). These include: 1. When there is an imbalance between supply and demand in the market; 2. To compete with market rivals by reducing production costs; 3. Greediness for higher profit margins; 4. A lack of trained labour using antiquated food processing techniques; and 5. Ignorance of disease outbreaks brought on by adulterated food products.

Food adulteration has emerged as one of the most severe issues in recent years and leading to major illnesses like cancer, asthma, and ulcers. The producers/farmers, manufacturers/enterprises, consumers, and the government all suffer greatly as a result of food adulteration (Asrat et al. 2012.,Gahukar ,2014 and Lakshmi et al. 2012).

Examples: Mixing of watch and starch powder (adulterant)in milk and curd (food products), mixing of Vanaspati /starch powder(adulterant) in ghee/cheese (food products),mixing chalk powder/starch powder(adulterant) in sugar(food products),mixing saw dust/dried leaves(adulterant) in tea powder(food products), leading to stomach disorders etc.

4.1.1. India laws related to food safety

The Food Safety and Standards Act of 2006 regulates the production, storage, distribution, sale, and importation of food products. The Food Safety and Standards Authority of India (FSSAI) was also created as a result. Additionally, it outlines the responsibilities of food manufacturers, wholesalers, distributors, sellers, and dealers. The following food laws were repealed and combined under the Food Safety and Standards Act, 2006 (FSS Act), which was passed in India.

1. The Prevention of Food Adulteration Act, 1954 (37 of 1954)
2. The Fruit Products Order, 1955.
3. The Meat Food Products Order, 1973
4. The Vegetable Oil Products (Control) Order, 1947
5. The Edible Oils Packaging (Regulation) Order, 1998.
6. The Milk and Milk Products Order, 1992

4.1.2. International organizations for food safety

1. World Health Organisation (WHO) - The Nutrition and Food Safety Team of the WHO monitors food safety and issues recommendations for preventing illnesses brought on by contaminated food. The responsibility for upholding food nutrition regulations falls on the Standards and Scientific Advice on Food and Nutrition (SSA) Unit of WHO.

2. Food and Agriculture Organisation (FAO) - Through the creation of more sustainable policies, it works to abolish hunger. It promotes businesses in sectors like agriculture, forestry, and fisheries to support the objectives and mission of the organisation.

3. Codex Alimentarius Commission (CAC) - Codex Alimentarius, which translates to "Food Code," is a compiling of Food Standards that have been ratified on an international level and is published by the Codex Alimentarius Commission (CAC). The standards covered cover a varied range of topics, such as food labelling, food safety, food additives etc.

4. International Organisation for Standardization (ISO) - Food products, food safety management, microbiology, fisheries, essential oils, starch, and its byproducts are all covered by ISO.

5. World Trade Organization (WTO) - This organisation prioritizes food standards over trade. The WTO has set some limitations since global food security is a significant issue.

4.2. Counterfeit products

Nowadays, counterfeiting is an extremely successful business. In order to capitalise on the brand value of the original product, counterfeit goods are made to look like the real thing. The majority of counterfeit goods come from the world's most commonly copied goods, which include apparel and footwear. Similar to how technology has advanced, India's economy has modernised and become more liberalised, which has given manufacturers and marketers the perfect platform and chance to misappropriate existing brands. Online shopping's rising popularity has also made it simpler to offer fake items. One of the markets with the highest growth for high-end luxury products is India. The anti-counterfeiting and brand protection summit of 2022 reported that the counterfeit market in India has crossed Rs. 40000 crores in the organised sector alone. The majority of Indian consumers prefer to purchase market-available counterfeit goods. According to Eisend and Guler (2006), price sensitivity, novelty seeking, status consuming, and peer pressure are the main variables affecting consumers' inclinations to buy counterfeit goods in India. Consumer attitudes and buy intentions in the fashion sector, especially in the Indian market, are significantly influenced by brand image, social considerations, and personality variables.

In order to capitalise on the reputation of legitimate companies, counterfeit brands are developed (Nordin, 2009; Bhatt and Reddy, 1998). The maker duplicates the logo and offers it for sale. Numerous thousands of individuals have occasionally died as a result of counterfeit products. The usage of narcotics and fake car components resulting in the death of people (Phau et al., 2001).

Example: Imitations of original items with low cost material mostly can be seen in clothing, fashion accessories, pharmaceuticals, automobile parts, software etc.

4.2. Indian laws related to anti counterfeit products

1. The Drugs and Cosmetics Act of 1940 creates mechanisms to combat the export of adulterated, fake, or misbranded medicines.
2. The Copyright Act of 1957, which offers statutory criminal approvals for copyright infringement, safeguards artistic, musical, theatrical, and literary works and also computer programmes.
3. The IT Act of 2000 was passed to regulate dishonest or criminal breaches committed utilising cutting-edge technology and modern computer systems.
4. According to the Trademarks Act of 1999, a registered trademark holder has the legal authority to sue an unregistered trademark for passing off.
5. A registered entity is permitted to use a design under the Designs Act of 2000. Any pattern, form, material, or colour or shape compositions that are advantageous to any thing or object are included in this.
6. The Food Safety and Standards Act of 2006 was passed to give government authorities the power to seize and destroy counterfeit goods that are misbranded and of poor quality.

For businesses that have registered their items as trademarks, counterfeiting can mean significant losses. Inappropriately made counterfeit goods can seriously hurt a trademark owner's business, jeopardising consumer safety and even their possible well-being. Trademark owners have the right, in accordance with the several Acts stated above, to take legal action in contradiction of any instances of trademark/copyright infringement they come across, however it cannot be entirely eradicated from the market.

4.3. Black-marketing and hoarding

An illicit supply and manufacture of goods and services that are outside the law is known as black marketing. When someone hoards, they buy a lot of something with the goal of storing it. People are enforced to tolerate this particular form of market monopoly. Purchase the same commodity with a different buyer because there is a lack of it. The idea of hoarding is connected to the black market in this way because such transactions are prohibited by law (Iqbal,2020).

To increase their profit by immoral business practises, people engaged in the hoarding business in the same way that they engaged in black marketing. This product is a fundamental good that many people utilise in trade. Hoarding is distinct from cartelization in that cartelization refers to a group of suppliers or manufacturers working together to try to restrict the supply of goods for a period of time so that, in the event of a shortage of that commodity, they can all monopolise the market and increase their profits by raising the prices of the goods.

Example: Black marketing and hoarding of medical supplies, agricultural products, essential comedies , sale of goods and services against the rules

4.3.1. Indian laws related to Black marketing and hoarding

1. The prevention of Black Marketing and Maintenance of Supplies of Essential Commodities Act, 1980 - provides for detention in cases for the purpose of preventing Black Marketing for Matters Connected thereto.
2. The Essential Commodity Act of 1955 make provisions for the control of the production, supply, and distribution of trade and commerce in commodities in the interest of the general public.
3. The 1940 pharmaceuticals and Cosmetics Act is a piece of consumer protection legislation that focuses on the standards and quality of pharmaceuticals produced in this country as well as the regulation of their import, production, sale, and distribution.
4. The Epidemic Diseases Act of 1897: This Act was created to stop the spread of potentially fatal epidemic diseases. The Epidemic Diseases Act's provisions were used when the coronavirus started to spread across the nation in March 2020, and numerous unethical and criminal actions were reported during the epidemic. People who were found to have committed these offences were also charged under other sections of the Indian Penal Code, such as section 405 for criminal breach of trust and section 420 for cheating, among others.

5. Conclusions

Consumers must be supported and cooperated by members of civil society and by government as well to make our country and its people more prosperous and progressive in consumer market. There are various legislations initiated by government to control malpractices by sellers. The government introduced new Consumer Protection Act, 2019 more powerful and effective than that of its older version (1986). Protecting customers' interests and rights is part of consumer protection.. There is also need of spreading awareness among the people regarding consumer rights and forms of exploitations. For effective consumer protection, it is imperative for three economic agents-consumers, businessmen and government of the economy to work together.

References

1. Abhirami, S., & Radha, R. (2015). Detection of food adulteration in selected food items procured by homemaker. *International Journal of Recent Scientific Research*, *6*(8), 5938-5943.
2. Aggarwal, VK. 2021.Consumer Protection: Law and Practice, Bharat Law House, Delhi..
3. Anita, G., & Neetu, S. (2013). Hazards of new technology in promoting food adulteration. *IOSR Journal of Environmental Science, Toxicology and Food Technology*, *5*(1), 08-10.
4. Asrat, A., Zelalem, Y., & Ajebu, N. (2012). Quality of fresh whole milk produced in and around Boditti, Wolaita, South Ethiopia. *The African Journal of Animal & Biomedical Sciences*, *7*(2), 95-99.
5. Bhat, S., & Reddy, S. K. (1998). Symbolic and functional positioning of brands. *Journal of consumer marketing*, *15*(1), 32-43.

6. Chatar, S.N., & Sanjay, K. (2020). Consumer protection in India: empowering consumer. *International Journal of Development Research.* 10 (02): 33873-33877.
7. Choudhary, A., Gupta, N., Hameed, F., & Choton, S. (2020). An overview of food adulteration: Concept, sources, impact, challenges and detection. *International Journal of Chemical Studies*, *8*(1), 2564-2573.
8. Eisend, M., and Schuchert-Guler, P. (2006). Explaining counterfeit purchases: A review and preview. *Academy of Marketing Science Review*, 12:1-22.
9. Gahukar, R. T. (2014). Food adulteration and contamination in India: occurrence, implication and safety measures. *International Journal of Basic and Applied Sciences*, *3*(1), 47.
10. Ganesan, G. and Sumathy, M. (2012).Globalisation and Consumerism: Issues and Challenges, Regal Publications, New Delhi.
11. Hamburg MA. Food and Drug Partnership for Safe Medicines Interchange.(2010). http://www.fda.gov/downloads/Drugs/ResourcesForYou/Consumers/BuyingUsingMedicineSafely/CounterfeitMedicine/UCM235240.pdf.
12. Iqbal, S.M.U. (2020). Hoarding and black-marketing during covid-19 Pandemic: an analysis of various statutory provisions to curb the problem. *Alochana Chakra Journal*.9(6):291-298.

13. Lakshmi ,V. 2012.Review article on food adulteration. *International Journal of Science Inventions Toady.* 1(2):106-113.

14. Manoj, K.Y.2020. Problems of consumers Protection in India: An overview. *Journal of Emerging Technologies and Innovative Research.*7(11): 1177-1179.

15. Narayan, D. Food Adulteration: Types, worldwide laws and futures. Health care. 2014. http://www.biotecharticles.com/Healthcare-Article/FoodAdulteration.

16. Nordin, F. (2009). Transcendental marketing: a conceptual framework and empirical examples. *Management Decision.* 47(10):1652-1664.

17. Phau., Sequeira, M. & Dix,S. (2001).Consumers willingness to knowingly purchase counterfeit products, *Direct Marketing: An International Journal.* 3(4):262-281.

18. Sahoo and Chatterjee. (2009). Consumer Protection - Problems and Prospects. *SSRN Electronic Journal.*7(7).

19. https://consumeraffairs.nic.in/acts-and-rules/consumer-protection retrieved on April 2023

20. https://www.indialawoffices.com/legal-articles/anti-counterfeiting-laws-in-india retrieved on March 2023

21. https://blog.ipleaders.in/hoarding-prohibition-law/ retrieved on April 2023

22. https://www.lawinsider.in/columns/black-marketing-and-hoarding-in-india-during-to-the-pandemic retrieved on May,2023

23. https://www.fssai.gov.in/cms/food-safety-and-standards-act-2006.php retrieved on April 2023
24. https://blog.ipleaders.in/indian-and-international-food-laws/ retrieved on May 2023
25. https://www.indiacode.nic.in/bitstream/123456789/7800/1/200634_food_safety_and_standards_act%2C_2006.pdf retrieved on April 2023
26. https://anticounterfeitingindia.com/ retrieved on May 2023

5.

HEALTH AND PSYCHOLOGICAL WELL-BEING

Dr. Alka Pandey and Dr. Shalini Kumari

*Assistant Professor, Department of Psychology, School of Liberal Education, Galgotias University, Uttar Pradesh, Plot No-2, Sector 17-A, Yamuna Expressway Greater Noida, Distt-Gautam Budh Nagar

Email: alka.tripathi86@gmail.com

Abstract

Nowadays, there is an increasing interest in achieving optimal physical and mental health, particularly in light of the uncertainties brought about by the Covid-19 pandemic. Consequently, the concept of well-being has gained significant attention in recent times. Present chapter offers a comprehensive analysis of various holistic well-being concepts and their correlation with the quality of life. This chapter explores the intricate relationship between health and psychological well-being, highlighting the impact of mental state on physical health and vice versa. It examines various studies and reviews that provide evidence for the interconnectedness of these two aspects of human well-being. The chapter aims to shed light on the importance of nurturing both physical and mental health to achieve a holistic state of well-being. This chapter, delve into the vital aspects of maintaining and enhancing both physical and mental well-being. The overall objective is to provide valuable insights and strategies for fostering a healthy lifestyle and promoting positive psychological states. By focusing on these fundamental elements, individuals can strive towards a balanced and fulfilling existence.

Keywords: Psychological well-being, Physical health, Mental health, Holistic well-being

1. Introduction

The correlation between physical health and psychological well-being constitutes a fundamental aspect of a well-rounded and satisfying life. While physical health pertains to the body's overall condition and its ability to function optimally, psychological well-being encompasses emotional, mental, and social dimensions. This symbiotic relationship profoundly shapes our perceptions, experiences, and coping mechanisms in the face of life's challenges and pleasures. The evolution of positive psychology has amplified the focus on psychological well-being across diverse fields (Henn et al., 2016; Hides et al., 2016), underscoring its significance. Attaining robust physical health and psychological well-being not only bolsters resilience in adversity but also cultivates contentment, self-awareness, and harmonious interpersonal connections. Prioritizing these aspects is pivotal for attaining comprehensive happiness and realizing our innate human potential.

2. The dynamic interaction of physical health and psychological well-being

The intricate interplay between physical health and psychological well-being has captivated researchers and healthcare professionals alike. This dynamic interaction holds far-reaching implications for overall well-being and happiness. The impact of physical health on psychological well-being is evident in various studies. For example, Revicki and Mitchell found that health-related problems were a primary source of strain among older adults (Revicki DA & Mitchell JP, Strain, 1990). Physical health significantly influences subjective well-being. Bishop et al. reported that diminished health was linked to lower morale (Bishop et al., 1986).

Physical health encompasses dimensions such as cardiovascular fitness, strength, flexibility, and freedom from illness. Conversely, psychological well-being encompasses emotional and mental states, including happiness, life satisfaction, resilience, and stress-coping abilities.

Numerous studies underscore the bidirectional nature of the connection between physical health and psychological well-being. It is widely acknowledged that regular physical activity and adopting a health-conscious lifestyle positively impact mental health. Exercise triggers the release of endorphins—known as "feel-good" hormones—contributing to elevated mood, stress reduction, and enhanced self-esteem. Research by Amy E Mitchell in 2018 corroborates bidirectional links between children's physical and psychological health. Dermatological conditions in children can affect psychological well-being, while psychological factors (like stress) can influence skin conditions.

Furthermore, physical activity has proven effective in alleviating anxiety and depression symptoms. Aerobic exercises, like running or swimming, stimulate the growth of new brain neurons, bolstering cognitive function and emotional well-being.

Conversely, poor physical health can adversely affect psychological well-being. Chronic illnesses, pain, or disabilities can evoke frustration, helplessness, and diminished life quality. These conditions may curtail engagement in once-enjoyable activities, compounding psychological distress.

Importantly, psychological well-being's impact on physical health is equally consequential. Individuals grappling with high stress, anxiety, or depression levels are more susceptible to physical health issues. Chronic stress can compromise the immune system, disrupt sleep, and contribute to cardiovascular diseases.

Recognizing the interwoven nature of physical health and psychological well-being underscores the need for a holistic healthcare approach. Integrating mental health support into primary care settings enhances comprehensive and effective treatment. Further, advocating regular exercise and healthy lifestyle choices proves pivotal in averting physical and psychological health disorders.

The synergy between physical health and psychological well-being is intricate and dynamic. Engaging in regular physical activity and adopting a health-conscious lifestyle positively impact mental health, while compromised physical health can exacerbate psychological distress. Acknowledging and addressing this synergy is pivotal in achieving overall well-being and promoting optimal health for individuals.

The intricate interconnection between physical health and psychological well-being underscores the foundation of a fulfilling life. The harmonious synergy of thoughts, emotions, and physical vitality forms a holistic framework that deeply impacts our overall health. When burdened with stress, negativity, or emotional turmoil, our minds can manifest these struggles as physical symptoms or compromised immune responses. Conversely, cultivating a positive mindset fosters better overall well-being, bolstering our ability to navigate life's challenges and promoting robust physical health. Embracing this profound relationship empowers us to cultivate a balanced fusion of mind and body, fostering equilibrium that nourishes not just our health, but our psychological vibrancy as well, resulting in a more enriching life journey.

3. The mind-body unity and its influence

The intricate link between the mind and body captivates researchers and healthcare professionals alike, offering a comprehensive perspective on human health. This interplay extends profound implications for well-being and happiness. The impact of physical health on psychological well-being is evident in studies. For example, Revicki and Mitchell discovered that health-related issues were a primary source of strain among older adults (Revicki DA & Mitchell JP, Strain, 1990). Physical health significantly influences subjective well-being. Bishop et al. reported that compromised health correlated with lower morale (Bishop et al., 1986).

Physical health encompasses diverse aspects such as cardiovascular fitness, strength, flexibility, and freedom from illness. Conversely, psychological well-being covers emotional and mental states including happiness, life satisfaction, resilience, and stress management.

Numerous studies highlight the mutual relationship between physical health and psychological well-being. Regular physical activity and adopting a health-conscious lifestyle have been correlated with improved mental health. Exercise triggers the release of endorphins—referred to as "feel-good" hormones—leading to enhanced mood, stress reduction, and increased self-esteem. Amy E Mitchell's 2018 research supports bidirectional links between children's physical and psychological health. Dermatological conditions can impact psychological well-being, and psychological factors (such as stress) can influence skin conditions.

Furthermore, physical activity alleviates symptoms of anxiety and depression. Aerobic exercises stimulate the growth of new brain neurons, enhancing cognitive function and emotional well-being.

Conversely, compromised physical health can adversely impact psychological well-being. Chronic illnesses, pain, or disabilities can evoke frustration, helplessness, and reduced life quality. These conditions may restrict engagement in previously enjoyed activities, heightening psychological distress.

Crucially, psychological well-being's influence on physical health should not be underestimated. High stress, anxiety, or depression levels render individuals more prone to physical health issues. Chronic stress can compromise the immune system, disrupt sleep, and contribute to cardiovascular diseases.

Recognizing the intertwined nature of physical health and psychological well-being advocates for holistic healthcare. Integrating mental health support into primary care settings enhances comprehensive and effective treatment. Further, promoting regular exercise and healthy lifestyle choices is pivotal in averting physical and psychological health disorders.

The interplay between physical health and psychological well-being is intricate and dynamic. Engaging in regular physical activity and adopting a health-conscious lifestyle positively influence mental health, while compromised physical health can exacerbate psychological distress. Acknowledging and addressing this interplay is pivotal in achieving overall well-being and promoting optimal health for individuals.

4. Benefits of psychological well-being on physical health

4.1. Physical health

Chronic pain, injuries, and illnesses can strain our coping abilities and induce stress. A balanced psychological well-being enhances resilience in dealing with such challenges, influencing their impact. It also guides us toward better self-care choices, mitigating the effects of chronic pain.

4.2. Mental health

A healthy psychological perspective fosters positive mental health and, consequently, overall health. A balanced psychological state contributes to a positive life outlook, which affects mental health, thereby influencing overall health.

4.3. Immune system

Effective stress management positively affects our immune system. Managing stress can reduce cortisol levels, impacting both mental and physical health positively.

5. Strategies for sustaining psychological well-being

5.1. Physical fitness:

Engaging in physical activity enhances psychological well-being by reducing stress and anxiety while elevating mood.

5.2. Mindfulness

Meditation and related practices aid stress management, enhancing emotional regulation.

5.3. Nutrition

A balanced diet rich in vitamins and minerals supports psychological well-being.

5.4. Sleep

Sufficient sleep enhances resilience to stress.

5.5. Social support

Strong social connections reduce loneliness and aid stress management.

5.6. Stress management

Effective stress management techniques contribute to emotional balance.

5.7. Professional help

Mental health professionals help address issues affecting psychological well-being.

6. Promoting stress management for holistic healing

Stress management is pivotal for both psychological and physical health. Effective stress management contributes to psychological well-being, thus positively affecting physical health. Managing stress reduces cortisol release, impacting mental and physical health positively. Stress negatively affects the immune system, making us prone to infection and impeding recovery from injury or illness. Effectively managing stress curtails its negative impact on physical health.

7. Lifestyle choices and their influence on psychological well-being

Our psychological well-being is closely tied to lifestyle choices. These choices can significantly impact mental health and overall contentment. Making healthy lifestyle choices positively impacts both psychological well-being and physical health. Balanced physical activity, nutritious diets, restful sleep, stress management, nurturing relationships, and self-care practices are key factors in achieving and maintaining psychological well-being.

8. Knowing when to seek professional help for physical healing

While numerous methods can enhance psychological well-being, seeking help might be necessary for effective change.

Difficulty in improving psychological well-being might indicate the need for professional assistance. Experiencing high stress levels, depression, anxiety, or negative impacts on physical health warrants professional support. Breaking the "feedback loop" of stress is vital; seeking help from friends, family, or professionals' aids in this process.

9. A balanced lifestyle's role in optimal health and resilience

In the modern world, sustaining a balanced lifestyle is paramount. Balancing physical, mental, and emotional well-being fosters optimal health and psychological resilience. Physical health is foundational, bolstered by regular activity, nutritious diets, and ample rest. Mental well-being thrives with practices like meditation and leisure activities. Emotional balance involves healthy emotional processing. Nurturing relationships, social connections, and managing stress all contribute to a balanced lifestyle, enhancing overall well-being and resilience.

The intricate connection between physical health and psychological well-being is undeniable. Fostering this connection empowers individuals to forge a harmonious fusion of mind and body, leading to a more enriching life journey.

10. Practical tips for achieving a balanced lifestyle

10.1. Prioritize self-care

Make time for activities that promote physical, mental, and emotional well-being, such as regular exercise, hobbies, and relaxation techniques.

10.2. Adopt a nutritious diet

Focus on consuming a balanced diet rich in fruits, vegetables, whole grains, lean proteins, and healthy fats.

10.3. Get adequate sleep

Aim for 7-9 hours of quality sleep per night to support physical and mental health.

10.4. Manage stress

Incorporate mindfulness practices, deep breathing exercises, or journaling into your daily routine to cope with stress effectively.

10.5. Stay socially connected

Foster and maintain relationships with friends, family, or community groups to build a strong support system.

10.6. Seek professional help

If you find yourself struggling with emotional or mental health challenges, do not hesitate to reach out to a qualified mental health professional.

11. Importance of psychological well-being to physical healing

Our psychological well-being is one of the most critical aspects of our physical health. A complex interplay between our mental, emotional, and physical health can impact our overall well-being.

When our psychological well-being is in balance, it can positively influence our physical healing. We may be able to better cope with physical pain, and our bodies may be more resilient when faced with illness or injury. When our psychological well-being is out of balance, it can harm our physical healing, making it harder to recover from injury or illness or manage chronic pain.

12. Practical strategies for attaining a balanced lifestyle

12.1. Prioritize Self-Care

Dedicate time to activities that nurture your physical, mental, and emotional well-being. Engage in regular exercise, pursue hobbies you enjoy, and practice relaxation techniques such as deep breathing or meditation.

12.2. Embrace a nutrient-rich diet

Opt for a balanced diet that includes a variety of fruits, vegetables, whole grains, lean proteins, and healthy fats. Nutrient-rich foods support both physical health and cognitive function.

12.3. Ensure quality sleep

Aim for 7-9 hours of uninterrupted sleep per night. Quality sleep is essential for physical recovery, cognitive function, and emotional resilience.

12.4. Manage stress mindfully

Incorporate mindfulness practices into your routine to manage stress effectively. Techniques like meditation, progressive muscle relaxation, or yoga can promote relaxation and emotional well-being.

12.5. Cultivate social connections

Maintain meaningful relationships with friends, family, and community members. Social connections provide emotional support and contribute to overall happiness.

12.6. Seek professional support

Don't hesitate to seek help from a qualified mental health professional if you're struggling with emotional or mental health challenges. They can offer guidance and strategies tailored to your needs.

13. The significance of psychological well-being in physical healing

Our psychological well-being holds immense importance in the realm of physical healing. The intricate interplay between our mental, emotional, and physical health significantly impacts our overall well-being.

A balanced psychological state positively influences our capacity for physical healing. It equips us to manage physical pain more effectively and enhances our body's resilience in the face of illness or injury. On the contrary, when our psychological well-being is disrupted, it can hinder physical healing, potentially prolonging recovery from injuries, illnesses, or chronic pain.

14. The importance of stress management for physical healing

Stress has a significant impact on our physical health, as well as our psychological well-being. Managing our stress is crucial to maintaining psychological well-being and, therefore, positively affects our physical health.

When we are stressed, the hormone cortisol is released. Being able to manage our stress can help us to reduce the amount of cortisol in our bodies. Less cortisol in our bodies can positively impact our mental and physical health.

When we are under stress, our immune system is negatively affected; it is less effective at fighting illness and healing from injury. This can make us more susceptible to infection, eg: a simple seborrheic dermatitis ear turning into a full-blown infection, and slow our recovery from injury or illness. Managing our stress helps us reduce the negative impact of stress on our physical health.

15. The impact of lifestyle choices on physical healing

Our psychological well-being and physical health are closely linked. This means that improving our psychological well-being can positively affect our physical health. Poor lifestyle choices can negatively impact our psychological well-being. This can harm our physical health. Making healthy lifestyle choices can boost both our psychological well-being and physical health.

16. When to seek professional help for physical healing

There are many ways to boost your psychological well-being, but we may have difficulty making changes. If someone struggle to improve their psychological well-being, it may be time to seek professional help.

When individual is experiencing high-stress levels, you may find it more challenging to reduce your stress. This can lead to what is known as a “feedback loop.” In this situation, stress leads to more stress leads to more stress. This can become a vicious cycle that is difficult to break. Finding a way to break the feedback loop can be helpful. Asking for help, whether from a friend, family member, or professional, is the best way to break the cycle. Despite the severity of these consequences, it is estimated that up to one-half of those with depression (Yung et.al., 2007 & Roy et.al., 2000) and only one third to one-half of those affected by anxiety disorders (Andrews et,al., 2001),seek professional help. Moreover, people often seek help from informal sources, such as friends or family rather than from formal sources such as doctors or psychologists (Rickwood, et.al. 1994 &Rickwood 2007) who can provide evidence-based treatments (Deane et.al. 2001). There is therefore a clear need to promote greater help-seeking from evidence-based sources.

17. Conclusions

Maintaining a balanced lifestyle is crucial for achieving optimal health and psychological resilience. The interconnectedness of physical, mental, and emotional well-being emphasizes the need to take a holistic approach to health. By prioritizing self-care, managing stress, and nurturing social connections, individuals can build resilience to better navigate life's challenges and lead a more fulfilling and joyful existence. A balanced lifestyle is a powerful tool for not only improving one's well-being but also for thriving in the face of adversity.

References:

1. Andrews G, Hall W, Teesson M, Henderson S. (1999), *The mental health of*

Australians. Commonwealth Department of Health and Aged Care, Mental Health Branch, Canberra.

2. Andrews G, Issakidis C, Carter G. (2001), Shortfall in mental health service utilization. *Br J Psychiatry*. **179**:417–425.
3. Bishop DS, Epstein NB, Keitner GI. (1986), Stroke: morale, family functioning, health status, and functional capacity. *Archives of Physical Medicine and Rehabilitation*. 67(2):84–87.
4. Deane FP, Ciarrochi J, Wilson C, Rickwood D, Anderson S. (2001*) Do high school students' intentions predict actual help seeking from school counselors? In 8th Annual Conference of Suicide Prevention*. Sydney, Australia.
5. Henn, C. M., Hill, C., and Jorgensen, L. I. (2016). An investigation into the factor structure of the Ryff Scales of Psychological Well-Being. S A. J. Ind. Psychol. 42, 1–12.
6. Hides, L., Quinn, C., Stoyanov, S., Cockshaw, W., Mitchell, T., and Kavanagh, D. J. (2016). Is the mental wellbeing of young Australians best represented by a single, multidimensional or bifactor model? Psychiatry Res. 241, 1–7.
7. https://medicine.wustl.edu/news/mind-body-connection-is-built-into-brain-study-suggests/
8. Kim ES, Sun JK, Park N, Kubzansky LD, Peterson C. (2013) *Purpose in life and reduced risk of myocardial infarction among older U.S. adults with coronary heart disease: a two-year follow-up. J Behav Med*. 36:124–133.
9. Revicki DA, Mitchell JP. Strain (1990), social support, and mental health in rural elderly

individuals. *Journals of Gerontology.* 1990;45(6):S267–S274.

10. Rickwood D, Deane F, Wilson C. (2007), *When and how do young people seek professional help for mental health problems? Med J Aust.* **187**(7 Suppl): S35–39.
11. Rickwood D, Braithwaite V. (1994), Social-psychological factors affecting help-seeking for emotional problems. *Social science & medicine (1982),* **39**(4):563–572.
12. Roy-Byrne PP, Stang P, Wittchen HU, Ustun B, Walters EE, Kessler RC. (2000), Lifetime panic depression comorbidity in the National Comorbidity Survey. Association with symptoms, impairment, course and help-seeking. *Br J Psychiatry.* **176**:229–235.
13. Yung AR, Killackey E, Hetrick SE, Parker AG, Schultze-Lutter F, Klosterkoetter J, Purcell R, McGorry PD, (2007) The prevention of schizophrenia. *International review of psychiatry (Abingdon, England)* **19**(6):633–646.

6.

EXTENSION EDUCATION IN THE MODERN ERA

Raman Bharti

Ph.D. Scholar

Department of Extension Education and Communication Management, College of Community and Applied Sciences, Maharana Pratap University of Agriculture and Technology, Udaipur, Rajasthan 313001

Email: khushboosargam@gmail.com

Abstract

Extension education is an essential component of the modern education system, which seeks to provide continuing education and training to people beyond the traditional classroom settings. In other words, extension education is a form of education that focuses on extending knowledge and skills beyond the traditional classroom setting to individuals, communities, and organizations. This chapter explores the concept of extension education and its importance in addressing societal needs and challenges. It discusses the various approaches and strategies used in extension education, such as field demonstrations, workshops, seminars, and mobile outreach programs. The chapter also highlights the benefits of extension education, such as increased knowledge and skills, improved productivity and efficiency, and enhanced quality of life.

Keywords: Extension, societal needs and approaches

1. Introduction

Extension education plays a vital role in bridging the gap between research and practice, and in disseminating knowledge, skills, technologies and information to farmers, rural communities, and other stakeholders. In the modern era, characterized by rapid technological advancements and changing socio-economic dynamics, extension education has undergone significant transformations to effectively address emerging challenges.

In today's rapidly evolving world, where knowledge and information are easily accessible, extension education plays a vital role in bridging the gap between academia and the wider community. Extension education, also known as outreach or continuing education, is a process that extends the knowledge and expertise of academic institutions to the general public, empowering individuals and communities to enhance their skills and improve their quality of life. It is a dynamic field that has evolved over time to meet the changing needs of society. In the modern era, extension education has experienced significant advancements, leveraging technological advancements and innovative approaches to enhance its effectiveness.

This chapter explores the evolution of extension education and highlights its key features, the significance of extension education, highlighting the challenges it faces and the strategies required to address them effectively, the role of extension education in the modern era, highlighting its strategies, challenges, and opportunities.

2. Definition and scope of extension education

Extension education is an outreach and educational process that bridges the gap between research institutions and end-users, primarily in agriculture, rural development, and community empowerment. It aims to improve the livelihoods and well-being of individuals and communities by providing them with relevant information, training, and resources. Extension education encompasses a wide range of activities, including workshops, field demonstrations, farm visits, ICT-based interventions, and social mobilization.

3. Evolution of extension education in the modern era

Extension education has evolved significantly over the years, adapting to the changing needs of society and the agricultural sector. Initially, extension services focused on transferring agricultural practices and technologies to farmers. However, in the modern era, extension education has expanded its scope to include a broader range of topics, such as sustainable agriculture, climate change adaptation, market-oriented farming, and rural entrepreneurship. This evolution reflects the growing recognition that extension education should encompass holistic development and empower communities to address multifaceted challenges.

Extension education has a rich history that dates back to the late 19th century when agricultural extension services were established to address the needs of farmers. Over time, the concept expanded beyond agriculture to encompass various fields such as health, nutrition, entrepreneurship, and community development. In the modern era, extension education has evolved to cater to the diverse needs of individuals and communities in a rapidly changing world.

3.1. Technological advancements

The modern era has witnessed rapid technological advancements that have revolutionized extension education. Information and Communication Technologies (ICTs) such as the internet, mobile phones, and social media have become powerful tools for extending knowledge and connecting with rural communities. ICT-based approaches, such as e-learning platforms, mobile applications, and online discussion forums, have enhanced the reach and accessibility of extension services.

3.2. Participatory approaches

Participatory approaches have gained prominence in extension education in the modern era. These approaches involve active involvement of farmers, community members, and other stakeholders in the design, implementation, and evaluation of extension programs. Participatory Rural Appraisal (PRA), Farmer Field Schools (FFS), and Community-Led Extension (CLE) are examples of participatory methods that promote knowledge sharing, experiential learning, and empowerment.

4. Role of technology in extension education

Technology has revolutionized the field of extension education, enabling the delivery of information and knowledge through various digital platforms. The internet, smart phones, and social media have become powerful tools for reaching a wider audience and engaging with learners in real-time. Online courses, webinars, and video tutorials have made education more accessible, allowing individuals to learn at their own pace and from anywhere in the world.

4.1. Reference in extension education

In the modern era, the importance of incorporating references and credible sources in extension education cannot be overstated. With the abundance of information available online, it is crucial to ensure that the knowledge being disseminated is accurate, reliable, and based on evidence. References provide learners with the opportunity to explore further, verify information, and build a deeper understanding of the subject matter. They also enable extension educators to maintain professional integrity and uphold the highest standards of education.

4.2. Credible sources and their evaluation

When incorporating references into extension education materials, it is essential to consider the credibility and reliability of the sources. Academic journals, books, government publications, and reputable websites are typically reliable sources of information. Peer-reviewed articles undergo rigorous scrutiny by experts in the field, ensuring the accuracy and validity of the information presented. Government publications often provide evidence-based guidelines and policies, while reputable websites are backed by authoritative institutions or experts in the respective fields.

4.3. Incorporating references in extension materials

Extension educators should incorporate references in their materials to provide learners with additional resources for further exploration. They can include a reference list at the end of their materials, citing the sources they have relied upon for the information presented. In addition, educators can include in-text citations when referring to specific studies or findings, allowing learners to locate the original sources and delve deeper into the subject matter.

5. Key features of extension education in the modern era

5.1. Participatory approaches

Modern extension education emphasizes the active participation of farmers and communities in the learning process. Participatory approaches, such as farmer field schools, participatory research, and community-based organizations, empower individuals to contribute their knowledge, share experiences, and collectively find solutions to problems. This approach ensures that extension services are demand-driven, context-specific, and responsive to the needs and aspirations of the target audience.

5.2. Information and communication technologies (ICTS)

The integration of information and communication technologies has revolutionized extension education. Digital platforms, mobile applications, and online resources provide instant access to relevant information, market prices, weather updates, and expert advice. ICTs also facilitate virtual learning, webinars, and remote consultations, enabling extension professionals to reach a wider audience and enhance the efficiency and effectiveness of knowledge dissemination.

5.3. Multi-disciplinary approaches

In the modern era, extension education has adopted a multi-disciplinary approach to address complex agricultural and rural development issues. Collaboration between extension professionals, researchers, policymakers, and practitioners from diverse fields, such as agronomy, economics, sociology, and environmental sciences, helps in developing integrated and sustainable solutions. This multidimensional perspective promotes a holistic understanding of the challenges and fosters innovative and context-specific interventions.

5.4. Inclusive and gender-responsive practices

Extension education in the modern era recognizes the importance of inclusivity and gender equality. Efforts are made to ensure the participation and engagement of marginalized groups, women, and youth in extension programs. Gender-responsive approaches acknowledge the unique roles, needs, and perspectives of men and women in agriculture and rural development, promoting equitable access to resources, information, and decision-making processes.

6. Challenges in extension education

6.1. Digital divide

While technology has transformed extension education, it has also exacerbated the digital divide. Limited access to technology, internet connectivity issues, and low digital literacy in rural areas pose challenges in reaching the intended beneficiaries. Efforts should be made to address these gaps and ensure equitable access to extension services.

6.2. Changing agricultural practices

Agricultural practices have evolved with advances in science and technology. Extension education needs to keep pace with these changes to provide relevant and up-to-date information to farmers. The rapid adoption of precision agriculture, agroecology, and sustainable farming practices requires extension professionals to continuously update their knowledge and skills.

7. The role of extension education in the modern era

7.1. Expanding access to education

In a digital age characterized by rapid technological advancements, extension education offers opportunities for lifelong learning to a diverse range of learners. By leveraging online platforms and innovative delivery methods, extension programs reach individuals who may have limited access to traditional education. The role of extension education in expanding access to education is further strengthened by collaborations with community organizations, government agencies, and businesses.

7.2. Meeting the needs of a changing workforce

The modern era is marked by a dynamic and evolving workforce, with new industries emerging and traditional job roles transforming. Extension education plays a crucial role in providing individuals with the skills and knowledge necessary to adapt to these changes. By offering professional development courses, certifications, and skill-building programs, extension education enables individuals to remain competitive and relevant in the job market.

7.3. Addressing societal challenges

Extension education goes beyond imparting knowledge; it actively engages with communities to address societal challenges. From promoting sustainable agriculture and environmental conservation to fostering entrepreneurship and empowering marginalized populations, extension programs play a pivotal role in creating positive social change. They facilitate the transfer of research findings and evidence-based practices to the community, enabling individuals to make informed decisions and contribute to their local and global contexts.

8. Challenges faced by extension education in the modern era

8.1. Technological Advancements and Digital Divide

While technology has opened up new avenues for extension education, it has also widened the digital divide. Not everyone has equal access to technology or the digital literacy skills required to participate fully in online learning. Extension programs need to be mindful of these disparities and employ strategies to ensure equitable access to education.

8.2. Engagement and retention

In an era of information overload, capturing and sustaining learners' attention is a significant challenge for extension education. Engaging learners through interactive and immersive learning experiences, gamification, and personalized learning pathways can enhance learner motivation and retention. Effective use of social media platforms and multimedia content can also amplify engagement and create vibrant learning communities.

8.3. Funding and sustainability

Extension education relies on adequate funding to maintain program quality and expand reach. However, securing sustainable funding can be challenging, as extension programs often compete with other priorities within educational institutions. Diversifying funding sources, seeking partnerships with external organizations, and demonstrating the societal impact of extension programs are strategies that can help ensure long-term sustainability.

9. Strategies for effective extension education in the modern era

9.1. Embracing Technology

Extension programs must embrace technological advancements and leverage digital tools to enhance accessibility and engagement. Online learning platforms, virtual reality, augmented reality, and mobile applications can facilitate flexible and interactive learning experiences. Integration of emerging technologies, such as artificial intelligence and machine learning, can enable personalized learning pathways and adaptive instruction.

9.2. Collaboration and partnerships

Collaboration between educational institutions, government agencies, community organizations, and industry stakeholders is essential for the success of extension education in the modern era. Partnerships can provide access to diverse expertise, resources, and funding opportunities. By collaborating with stakeholders, extension programs can align their offerings with the needs of the target audience. Employing data analytics and learning analytics can provide insights for evidence-based decision-making and enhance program quality.

10. Opportunities in extension education

10.1. Big data and analytics

Big data and analytics have the potential to revolutionize extension education by providing insights and predictions for decision-making. Analysing large volumes of data on weather patterns, market trends, and farmer profiles can help extension professionals tailor their services, provide customized advice, and identify emerging needs.

10.2. Climate change adaptation

Extension education plays a crucial role in building resilience and helping farmers adapt to climate change. By providing information on climate-smart agriculture, sustainable land management, and water conservation practices, extension professionals can support farmers in mitigating the impacts of climate change and improving their productivity.

11. Conclusions

Extension education has adapted to the challenges and opportunities of the modern era by embracing participatory approaches, leveraging information and communication technologies, adopting multi-disciplinary perspectives, and promoting inclusivity and gender equality. By incorporating these key features, extension professionals can effectively empower farmers and rural communities, enhancing their resilience, productivity, and well-being. Continued research, innovation, and collaboration will be crucial in further advancing extension education to meet the evolving needs of the agricultural sector in the dynamic landscape of the modern era.

References

1. Chambers, R. (1997). Whose reality counts? Putting the first last. Intermediate Technology Publications.
2. FAO. (2011). Gender in agriculture sourcebook. Food and Agriculture Organization of the United Nations.
3. Vanclay, F., Lawrence, G., & Lockie, S. (Eds.). (2013). Agricultural extension and rural development: Breaking out of traditions. Routledge.
4. Qamar, M. K., & Qureshi, S. E. (Eds.). (2016). E-Agriculture and Rural Development: Global Innovations and Future Prospects. Springer.
5. Boeren, E., van der Rijst, R. M., & Wals, A. E. (2017). Exploring the potential of citizen science for nature-based solutions in cities. Sustainability Science, 12(6), 927-939.
6. McLaughlin, J. D., & Healy, R. G. (2016). Digital badging in higher education and its impact on the traditional model of the university. Journal of Research on Technology in Education, 48(1), 1-15.
7. Rumble, G. (2019). The costs and benefits of online and distance learning. Routledge
8. Smith, L., & Booth, S. (2019). Extension education: Principles and practice. CABI.

9. Vasilj, M., & Vasilj, I. (2020). Adaptive e-learning: A review of the literature and a small-scale content review. Journal of Computing in Higher Education, 32(2), 273-291.
10. Davis, C. A., & Khurana, V. (Eds.). (2018). Advances in Agricultural Extension Education: Global Perspectives. Routledge.
11. OECD. (2018). Education at a Glance 2018: OECD Indicators. OECD Publishing.
12. Chambers, R. (2014). Participatory extension: The next step for agricultural development. London, UK: Routledge.
13. Reddi, U. V. (2019). Modernizing Agricultural Extension Education. Indian Journal of Agricultural Extension and Rural Development, 27(2), 161-170.
14. United States Department of Agriculture. (2017). Agricultural Extension Education: International Perspectives. Nova Science Publishers.
15. Chambers, R. (2014). Participatory extension: The next step for agricultural development. London, UK: Routledge.
16. Kumar, R., & Ranjan, M. (2020). Technological interventions in extension education: Opportunities and challenges. Journal of Extension Education, 32(2), 15-22.
17. Mishra, S., & Choudhary, A. (2022). Big data analytics in agriculture: Opportunities and challenges for extension education. Computers and Electronics in Agriculture, 197, 107319.
18. Qiang, C. Z., & de Silva, H. (2019). Bridging the digital divide: Measuring digital literacy. World Bank Research Observer, 34(2), 223-247.

19. Rezaei-Moghaddam, K., & Pardakhti, M. (2019). Climate change adaptation in agriculture: The role of extension education. Journal of Agricultural Education and Extension, 25(1), 1-16.
20. Smith, J., & Johnson, L. (2018). Extension education: Concepts, practices, and emerging trends. New York, NY: Routledge.
21. Srinivasan, V., & Darr, S. (2021). Advancing extension education for the future of agriculture. Journal of Agricultural Education and Extension, 27(1), 1-4.

7.

A PARADIGM SHIFT IN EXTENSION APPROACHES FOR SUSTAINABLE RURAL DEVELOPMENT

Seema Chawla[1], Pooja Gaba[2]

[1]Assistant Professor, Krishi Vigyan Kendra Sriganganagar, (Swami Keshwanand Rajasthan Agricultural University), Rajasthan; com [2]Creative Head, Craftales, New Delhi

Email: seemachawladr@gmail

Abstract

The extension system's concept, philosophy, and methodology have undergone significant transformations in the age of globalisation. In order to meet the emerging challenges, there is need to develop symbiotic and rational strategy for enhancing crop productivity and providing livelihood options to the rural masses. Upcoming opportunities and challenges enforce task of a different perspective, where in extension needs to reorient and revitalize itself to strengthen the nation's initiative for its prosperity. Reorientation of extension approaches is much needed to help people to help themselves with capacity building among the farming community and required a thorough analytical review of the existing approaches to extension. Present extension tactics had lost their proficiency to chalk out the path of sustainable rural development. After Independence, a number of strategies have been followed to enhance rural community participation in form of CAD, IADP, NDP, SFDA, IRDP, Training and Visit system for employment generation in agriculture and allied sectors. These approaches played not well due to lack of active participation and involvement of farmers while designing the technologies. In view to bridge the gap between policy makers and farmers, IVLP and ATMA came into existence with bottom-up planning and participatory methodologies.

Although these approaches have resulted in increased agriculture potential and promoted participation of rural people for sustainable development yet the individual oriented extension strategy overlooked the needs of collective masses. In light of this perspective, this review paper take into account the missing links, document the experiences and suggest dynamic extension strategies to build up the development competencies among the farming audience to empower them for sustainable rural development.

Keywords: Extension approaches, sustainable development.

1. Introduction

India's historical and wide spread agriculture extension system has dominant agricultural and rural development goals at every step of its evolution period. These goals were achieved by the extension system which is traditionally funded, managed and delivered by the public sector. Although the share of agriculture in Gross Domestic Product (GDP) has been declining over the years yet agriculture sector has an influential long term record of taking our country out from critical food deficits despite rapid population shoot up. The credit factor behind the success was heavy reliance on the activities of pluralistic extension system. Agricultural extension system operates through the Ministry of Agriculture, ICAR,SAU's, State departments of agriculture, ATMA,KVKs and other extension agencies like Cooperative federations, NGO's etc. A wide gap exists between the technology developed / and the technology disseminated/ adopted by farming audience. The first line extension pillars such as KVKs and ATMA are emphasizing continuously on quality human resources to catch the needs of farming community. Extensive efforts of extension professionals require a shift from technology dissemination to technology application mode to intensify the extension efforts. In addition to this various challenges are floating in front of extension expertise and policy makers such as lack of synchronisation between technical knowledge and prevailing extension skills, less number of trained extension professionals, rapidly changing rural resources, diversified economic sphere of rural people and climatic changes ultimately.

The biggest challenge with extension is to modify and strengthening of pluralistic agriculture extension and advisory system towards the broader aim of uplifting the rural livelihood and increasing the farm income. These rising issues and challenges enforce the task, where in extension system needs to be reoriented and revitalize its approaches and strategies to strengthen the nation's primitive goal of sustainable development. Reorientation of extension approaches is much needed to develop capacity building among the farming community and required a detailed review of the existing approaches as these had lost their proficiency to chalk out the path of viable rural development.

In light of these factual facts there is an urgent need for a comparative analysis of different extension approaches to get the way of success to development agricultural extension. Proper awareness about the different extension approaches and effective implementation at grass root level will definitely result in income and employment generation among the rural masses. Before knowing about extension approaches, here is a view about the concept of agricultural extension approach.

2. The concept of agricultural extension approach

Agricultural Extension Approach denotes the dominant instructional guide and way of action to an extension system or organization to achieve the desired goals and objectives so efficiently.

It is the philosophy or doctrine for the extension system which evokes, energises and guides such aspects of the whole system as its structure, dynamics leadership and resources with its liaison links. It presents dominant facts in extension management and administration. It affects the planning, content, selection of methods, target fixing and participation of audience, prioritization of resources and its allocation with monitoring and evaluation of extension activities

3. Criteria for identifying appropriate extension approaches

For selecting and designing any extension approach seven factors should be kept in mind as follows:

3.1. Dimensions of extension approaches

- The Identified problem
- The purpose (supposed to attain)
- Way to control programme planning
- Prospects of field professionals
- Resources Required
- Implementation Techniques
- The outputs to measure success

4. Types of extension approaches

The extension approach is a beginning point to start an action, not the end point. Following are the various extension approaches which has been practised by the extension personnel over the years to get the objective of sustainable during development rural development:

- The General Agriculture Extension Approach
- The Commodity Specialized Approach
- The Educational Institution Extension Approach
- The Project Approach
- Transfer of Technology Approach

- The Farming Systems Research Extension(FSR-E) Approach
- The Cost Sharing Approach
- Participatory Agricultural Extension Approach
- Participatory Action Models (PAM) Approach
- Cooperative Self- help Approach
- Integrated Training approach

4.1. The general agriculture extension approach

The most prevalent extension approach in the world is the general agriculture extension approach. This approach embodies that technology and knowledge which is suitable for localities but they are not using them. This approach is a centralised and government controlled venture. This focuses on the felt needs of the clientele group to increase production level and to give them improved way to quality life. The key ingredients of this approach is its recognition of broader view of agricultural and rural development goals like Farm management, Household economic analysis, Conservation of soil strata etc.

4.2. The commodity specialized approach

The approach works with one special or particular crop or commodity which is highly specialized for a particular area. Most of the time this enforces the export crops such as coffee, sugar, tobacco, cotton or rubber etc. The main focus of this approach is groups working for product extension, input facility, produce marketing and price-fixation facility. On the other hand, it encompasses other aspects of farming as livestock, dairy, fishery, irrigation or fertilizer occasionally. The major objective of this approach is to enhance the marketing and production of high values and commodities more efficiently and timely. Farmers are motivated to participate in view of profit sharing which boost their farm income and inclined them to technology acceptance.

4.3. The educational institution extension approach

This approach works with dynamic participation of agricultural schools, colleges and Universities with this assumption that these educational institutions have technical-sound knowledge, which is useful and important to rural farm people. The main aim of this approach is to make these people proficient about scientific agriculture. Although, agricultural extension is not typically their primary role, yet these provide technical knowledge and research ability to enrich rural people. The major emphasis is on transfer of technical knowledge efficiently among them.

4.4. The project approach

With reference to Project approach, main thrust is on the fact that if we want to procure better anticipated results, then large numbers of resources are to be invested in a particular location within a stipulated time frame. As this approach concentrates on a fixed time frame, hence continuity in final results is anticipated and well-ensured. One bigger advantage of this approach is that successful methods and project techniques can be replicated to another similar locations and available resources to catch the confirmed results after the completion of project. The major theme is to show the technology demonstration to the clientele, to be accomplished in fixed time period. Success of Project can be assessed frequently to enforce further implementation.

4.5. Transfer of technology approach

The best known extension approach to transfer the advanced technologies to the ultimate audience is the transfer of technology approach which is majority of top-down approach. By this approach subject matter specialists/ experts /scientists tries to find solution of farmer's major technological problems at their research stations. This extension approach is being used since years and found very effective in various circumstances to equip people with sustainable agriculture. By this approach we can enhance and rectify the accountability of extension professionals. The positive outcomes are regular farm visits, frequent and regular trainings of extension workers. It is a professional approach, emphasizing extension activities by systematic concentrated efforts through training and visit program for the rural farm people. It enforces the farmers to get first hand problem-oriented guidance from extension professionals. It creates dynamic linkage between farmers, professional extension officials and researchers for better future of agriculture.

4.6. The farming systems research extension (fsr-e) approach

The Farming systems Research and Extension Approach (FSR-E) is a way for agricultural research and development that perceives the whole farm as a system and emphasize on inter- woven relationship of different components under the pursuance of a single household members. The main focus of this approach is to improvise the well-being of an individual farmer or its family in view of both personal and social goals, concentrating on constraints and potentials of the farming system. With the perception of viewing farming system, as a complete closed unit means this approach studies all the relevant facts of individual household by regular visits, identify their problems, opportunities and fix the priority level accordingly. Recognition of linkage results in the development of whole farming system.

This FSR-E approach is very effective as it is a farmer centered approach which is:-

- Problem solving
- Comprehensive
- Interdisciplinar
- Complementary
- Interactive
- Dynamic
- Responsible

The main feature of this approach is holistic and system oriented. Farmers are involved at each and every step of problem identification and solving process. This approach bridge the gap between research experiments and technology reach of farmers. The sole purpose of FSR-E approach is to generate more suitable and apt technologies for clientele farmers and to rectify the policies. It supports services to raise farm production and boost the identified goals of society. By pursuing the FSR-E approach, extension professionals can meet out the needs and interests of the local farm people by research interventions according to the available farming system conditions.

4.7. The cost sharing approach

The cost sharing approach have the basis of doing work where local people are not able to solve their problems and issues itself, hence are willing to pay for the agricultural development. In this approach cost of agricultural extension is shared between the local people (the clients) and agricultural professionals. Another principle is to make funding of agricultural extension available, feasible, affordable and sustainable at both levels- central and local levels. The main purpose is to provide and facilitate self improvement of farming community through shared resources and cost. The ethics of this approach lies in the fact that the selected program is more likely to suit local resources, situations and people's interests of the selected area. In turn, it helps the farmers to know about self-improvement and development through shared resources.

Participatory Agricultural Extension Approach

Simply participatory approach denotes that an individual responsible for solving a problem or designing an innovation encourages people to participate who and directly related to the results of the concerned works. Thus in prospect of agricultural extension, this approach concentrates the felt needs of the clientele farmers to enhance the production level and quality of life. The approach works on the assumption that farming audience has much wisdom and way of thinking but prevailing living circumstances could be improved by inculcating outside resources and services. It further reinforces the assumption that participatory extension has a positive effect as it is based on group learning and group action. Participation of farmers results into efficient extension system and efforts. Through this approach, planning of programmes can be controlled by local people often by some informal groups such as farmer's association, community groups etc. In execution of extension program, group meetings and interactive demonstrations are held on the farmer's field and related queries are resolved on the spot by the extension professionals. Implementation is made effective through group meetings, group and individual discussions and interactive sessions. In turn, success or failure is measured through the number of beneficiaries or clientele farmers actively participating in the running program and continue to participate in the coming extensions programs by suggesting strategies and policies of work to be undertaken. In nutshell, farmers or their representatives participating in each and every era of work assigned, from planning to implementation and evaluation is the core theme of this approach.

4.8. Participatory action model (PAM) approach

Participatory Action Model (PAM) is a managerial approach where all related extension agencies, farmers groups and individual farmers having common interest and development initiative, come together to form a common platform which facilitate problem solving jointly and promote action for mutual benefits. This approach works on the principle of work convergence to divergence means common interests are focused on specific issues and group plans are executed to utilize the momentum gained through group activities.

4.9. Cooperative self- help approach

The Cooperative self- help approach works on the principle that rural transformation must start with the changes in the rural people themselves so that outside resources were utilized to help them towards the express needs of the people. The changes may be in terms of attitudes, inspirations and perceptions of themselves. Local institutions or societies are enforced for cooperative self-help among people. Under the approach, village people select their chairperson on the basis of their expertise and technical skills organize the cooperative group, registered their society and maintain proper records to adopt improved agriculture practices by regular interactive session among members.

4.10. Integrated training approach

This approach emphasizes on acquiring the systematic and intensive skills which are specific and precise to the subject and technology transmission .In this approach, learners are assembled at a training centre for a particular defined period for transmitting instructions. After getting training and proficiency in specific skills, trained extension professionals are supposed to transfer the acquired skills to the rural people towards the way of sustainable rural development.

5. Conclusions

Over the years a number of extension and development approaches were implemented to speed up the agriculture production productivity and improvement in quality of life of rural audience. After Independence, a number of strategies have been followed to enhance rural community participation in form of CAD, IADP, NDP, SFDA, IRDP,

Training and Visit system for employment generation in agriculture and allied sectors. These approaches played not well due to lack of active participation and involvement of farmers while designing the technologies. In view to bridge the gap between policy makers and farmers, IVLP, KVKs and ATMA came into existence with bottom-up planning and participatory methodologies.

In spite of all these efforts, public extension system is in search of fresh extension approaches to boost the agriculture development with bottom up planning. Role of public- private extension has been reorganised in implementation of different rural development programs so it is a serious concern of matter to work out an integrated extension approach to guard needs and interest of the farm people. Precisely, our extension system needs to develop a synergistic and coherent approach to enhance crop production and providing livelihood sustainability to the rural masses. For this purpose, documentation of all the relevant extension approaches should be taken into account by the extension experts, policy planners and stakeholders to strengthen the community development extension system.

References

1. Benson T. and Petros C. (2022) Climate-Smart Agricultural Extension Service Innovation Approaches in Uganda: Review Paper. International Journal of Food Science and Agriculture, 6(1), 35-43. DOI: 10.26855/ijfsa.2022.03.006.
2. K. Davis. (2019). "The complex processes of agricultural education and extension." Taylor & Francis, 2019

3. Kareem M.A and Phand S. (2018) :Extension Approaches and Methods Adopted by the Agri-Allied Sector Departments of Maharashtra State, *Journal of Agricultural, Biological and Environmental Sciences* Vol.05 : 19-29
4. Kromah,A. (2016):Extension Approaches in Agricultural Extension https://meas.illinois.edu/wp-content/uploads/2016/03
5. Singh, K. M. (2018): Modern Extension Approaches for Livelihood Improvement for Resource Poor Households. https://mpra.ub.uni-muenchen.de/104304/MPRA Paper No. 104304,

8.

COMPUTER AIDED DESIGNING IN TEXTILE AND APPAREL INDUSTRY: WITH REFERENCE TO FASHION EDUCATION

Dr. Bindu Chaturvedi[1], Nikita Sachwani[2]

1Professor and Head, [2]Research Scholar (JRF)

Department of Garment Production and Export Management

Government Arts Girls College, Kota

University of Kota, Kota

Email: binduchaturvedi71@gmail.com

Abstract

Computer-aided designing (CAD) has emerged as a powerful tool in the textile and apparel industry, transforming various aspects of design creation, production, and innovation. This research aims to explore the utilization of CAD software in the context of fashion education investigating its impact on the teaching and learning processes, as well as its potential implications for industry requirements and skill development.

This research comprehensively investigates the features, benefits, required technical skills, pricing, and variety of CAD software available, as well as their applications within the textile, apparel, and fashion sectors. For inclusion of CAD software in academic curricula, factors such as software availability, licensing terms and conditions, user interface, and training facilities for students and staff members are identified as key factors. Additionally, the study conducts a comparative analysis of the technical requirements within the industry and the training provided by educational institutions to students. By examining the gaps between industry expectations and academic offerings, the research aims to identify areas for improvement and propose measures to bridge these gaps.

The findings of this study will contribute to the understanding of the impact of CAD in fashion education and its relevance to the evolving needs of the industry. The research outcomes will inform curriculum development, pedagogical strategies, and training programs, ensuring that fashion education keeps pace with technological advancements and equips students with the necessary skills to excel in the contemporary textile and apparel landscape.

Keywords: computer-aided designing, CAD software, textile and apparel industry, fashion education, curriculum development, skill development.

1. Introduction

Computer-aided design, commonly known as CAD, refers to the involvement of specifically designed software and computer systems to create, modify, and visualize designs in a virtual environment. It came into existence because of the need for more efficient, accurate, and flexible design processes. Demand for faster iterations and the desire for enhanced collaboration contributed to the development and adoption of CAD in various industries. The roots of CAD can be traced back to the early 1960s when computers first began to be used in design and engineering fields. However, it wasn't until the 1980s that CAD started to gain widespread adoption in the textile and apparel industry. The need for constant innovation and increase in efficiency to meet the ever-evolving demands of consumers led to the integration of technology in the form of computer-aided design (CAD), which has revolutionized the way design and production processes are approached and has brought in a significant transformation in the industry, enabling designers to work more efficiently and explore new possibilities in design creation.

During its initial years, CAD systems were primarily used by large companies with extensive resources due to the high cost of hardware and software. Designers gradually shifted from traditional hand-drawn sketches and manual pattern-making techniques to digital design platforms. CAD empowered designers with an ability to create intricate and complex designs with precision and accuracy. The software provided a wide range of tools and features that allowed designers to sketch, draft, and render their ideas digitally. This digital representation allowed for easy manipulation and modification of designs, reducing the time and effort required compared to traditional methods.[11]

2. CAD for fashion, apparel and textile: present scenerio

As technology advanced, CAD software became more sophisticated, offering features such as three-dimensional modeling, fabric simulation, and rendering capabilities. Over the years, CAD has become an indispensable tool in the fashion and apparel sector. Companies, while selecting softwares and related systems consider their requirement as per current and future requirements of expansion in production, budget versus the expected return by use of such technology, Hardware and Software requirements and their availability, ease of operation with respect to user interface and availability of timely expert assistance in case of technical issues so that the production does not suffer.

A plethora of CAD software options is available worldwide to cater to the specific needs of the textile, fashion, and garment industry. These software packages vary in terms of functionality, user interface, compatibility, and pricing. In India, where the fashion industry is thriving, several popular CAD software options are widely used. Some of the prominent CAD software packages in India, such as C Design Fashion, PatternSmith, Optitex, Lectra Modaris (pattern design), Gerber AccuMark, Adobe Illustrator, Coral Draw while CAD software options for textile designing include TexGen (2D and 3D weave design), Texronic (carpet design, weave design- Jacquard and Dobby), JacqCAD, DigiFab (Digital printing on textiles), Arahne and Textile Vision (colour management, product price calculation, yarn consumption calculation, Fabric simulation in three dimensional plane). These software solutions have price ranges that typically range from INR 2,00,000 to INR

10,00,000 or more, depending on the software package and licensing options.

2.1. Skills required to operate these software are as follows

S. No.	CAD Software	Skills Required
1.	C Design Fashion[16]	• Understanding of C Design Fashion's interface, tools, and functionalities. • Familiarity with the software's brush, pen, and shape tools to create accurate and detailed fashion illustrations. • Understanding of digital textile design and the ability to create patterns and prints. • Color and texture manipulation • Skills in arranging design elements, balancing proportions, and creating visually appealing layouts for fashion design presentations. • Knowledge of garment construction and the ability to create technical drawings and specifications. • Collaboration and file management.
2.	Pattern Smith[22]	• Proficiency in pattern-making techniques, including creating and modifying 2D patterns.

		• Understanding of grading, marker making, and nesting functionalities- adding annotations, grain lines, notches, and other important details that communicate construction and assembly information to manufacturers or pattern makers. • Knowledge of garment construction and the ability to generate accurate pattern pieces for production.
3.	Optitex [9]	• Proficiency in patternmaking and 2D pattern development. • Ability to create and modify 3D virtual prototypes and simulate fabric draping • Simulating different fabric textures and properties • Developing proper fit with Optitex tools. • Knowledge of grading, marker making, and nesting for efficient material utilization.
4.	Lectra by Modaris [20]	• Used for pattern design, grading, digital prototyping. • Familiarity with the software's pattern-making tools and functionalities. • Proficiency in 2D pattern development and grading.

		• Understanding of garment fit and the ability to create and modify patterns for different sizes.
5.	Astor's 'REDTREE'[2]	• **First and only *MADE IN INDIA* CAD solution.** • Complete production management software. • Less laborious pattern making. Patented technology develops basic patterns for a variety of design by just entering measurements as input. • Knowledge of entire garment manufacturing process. • Digital designing and marker plan analysis skills required. • Knowledge of pattern grading.
6.	Gerber AccuMark[7]	• Used in the fashion and apparel industry, primarily for pattern making, marker making, and production planning • Knowledge of grading, marker making, and automated nesting for efficient material utilization. • Understanding of technical specifications and the ability to generate production-ready pattern files.
7.	Gemini[5]	• For pattern making, grading, and marker making in the fashion and apparel

		industry Skills:- • Basic computer skills are essential, including familiarity with operating systems (such as Windows) • Understanding of pattern making, grading, and marker making concepts in the context of the fashion and apparel industry • Knowledge of garment construction, measurements, and sizing principles • Knowledge of CAD principles, terminology, and workflows • Ability to digitize and input existing paper patterns • Understanding of grading techniques • Knowledge of marker making concepts
8.	Adobe Illustrator[13]	• Ability to create accurate and detailed digital drawings and sketches using the drawing tools in Adobe Illustrator. • Editing vector-based objects such as lines, shapes, and curves to create fashion illustrations, technical drawings, and flat sketches. • Designing skills to be able to create

		digital swatch, gradient, pattern library. Fabric texture simulation. • Understanding of text tools to add labels, annotations, and descriptions to your fashion designs, and explore typography options for creative effects.
9.	CorelDRAW[18]	• Ability to create accurate and detailed digital drawings and sketches using CorelDRAW's drawing tools. • Ability to manipulate and edit vector-based objects such as lines, shapes, and curves to create fashion illustrations, technical drawings, and flat sketches • Expertise in the use of color palettes, color swatches, gradients, and color harmonies to create visually appealing and harmonious color schemes. • Knowledge of fashion design principles, garment construction techniques, and industry trends
10.	Audaces[4]	• Proficiency in creating new digital patterns from scratch and modifying existing patterns • Understanding and application of grading techniques within Audaces software. • Knowledge of marker making concepts and the ability to optimize fabric

		utilization by creating efficient marker layouts. • Familiarity with technical drawing tools and functions in Audaces software. This includes creating technical flats, annotations, measurements, and other technical details necessary for pattern production. • Simulating fabric draping, texture, and other visual effects to visualize the final garment design.
11.	TukAcad[12]	• Pattern Digitization • Pattern Creation and Modification • application of grading techniques within TukAcad software • Marker Making, Technical Drawing • Ability to edit existing markers, add or remove pattern pieces, and optimize marker layouts for improved fabric utilization and production efficiency. • Familiarity with the automated cutting features in TukAcad software, which allow for precise and efficient fabric cutting based on the digital patterns and markers created.
12.	Morgan Tecnica[21]	• Familiarity with the software interface, navigation, and functionalities to

13.		efficiently operate the software. • Knowledge of computer-aided design (CAD) and computer-aided manufacturing (CAM) principles. • Skill in digitizing patterns. • Pattern Editing and Manipulation • Skill in creating efficient markers. • Skill in adjusting marker layouts, adding or removing patterns, and fine-tuning the marker for improved material efficiency. • Managing fabrics and materials within the software as well as managing material consumption and inventory. • Understanding of compatibility of Morgan Tecnica software with different cutting machines. • Skill in collaborating with other departments, such as Collaboration with departments such as design, production, and logistics, and effectively communicating and sharing information between different software and systems necessary when Morgan Tecnica software is integrated into the larger production workflow.
13.	CLO3D and CLO5[10]	• Familiarity with 3D garment design principles

		• Understanding garment construction, pattern-making, and fitting concepts • understanding the software's capabilities • Ability to create and manipulate patterns within the software is a key skill. • Skill in applying fabric properties, simulating drape, stiffness, and texture, and understanding how different fabrics behave in virtual garments • Proficiency in incorporating garment detailing and trim details and accurately representing their placement, functionality, and visual appearance enhances the realism of the virtual garments. • Skill in analyzing and interpreting fit issues • Skills in applying realistic lighting, textures, colors, and materials • Understanding the software's role within the overall design and production workflow
Textile Design Specific Softwares		
14.	TexGens	• 2D and 3D weave designing • Understanding of textile weave

		structures. • Knowledge of fabric properties • Ability to simulate different weaving patterns
15.	Texronic[24, 25, 26]	• Used for carpet design, weave design - Jacquard and Dobby Skills: - • Proficiency in creating designs using Jacquard and Dobby techniques. • Understanding of carpet construction • Precise visualisation to create accurate designs for manufacturing.
16.	.JacqCAD[3]	• Familiarity with the software's Jacquard weaving functionalities. • Proficiency in designing and modifying complex Jacquard patterns. • Knowledge of textile weaving techniques and the ability to simulate fabric draping.
17.	DigiFab (Digital printing on textiles)	• Understanding of digital textile printing processes and color management. • Proficiency in creating digital print designs, patterns, and repeats. • Knowledge of fabric types and printing techniques to optimize design

		outcomes.
18.	Textile Vision[27]	• Familiarity with the software's interface and tools for textile design. • Creating and modifying textile patterns, prints, and colorways. • Understanding of fabric properties. • Ability to simulate different fabric textures and finishes.

Above was a comprehensive discussion about the features, benefits, required technical skills, pricing, and variety of CAD software available, as well as their applications within the textile, apparel, and fashion sectors. As the requirements of designers and other experts for the industry must be fulfilled by fashion education institutions, inclusion of CAD in fashion curriculum is of great importance. Curriculum also needs to be updated with industry needs to ensure appropriate employment opportunities to their students. Inclusion of CAD in educational curriculum requires careful consideration of factors such as software availability, licensing terms and conditions, user interface, and training facilities for students and staff members and budget constraints. Software providers offer cost-effective packages tailored to accommodate the budget constraints of educational institutions. These discounted pricing options are an attempt to make CAD software accessible for education curriculum, helping students in gaining hands-on experience.

Currently specific software from Adobe Creative Cloud (formerly known as Adobe Creative Suite) Package namely,

Adobe Photoshop[15], Adobe Illustrator, Adobe InDesign along with Corel Draw software[15, 8], TukAcad[28], CLO 3D, CLO 5 are the most seen as part of curriculum in India. SketchUp are also part of curriculum but not specifically for designing.

3. Most popular academically used CAD softwares at a glance

Basis of Comparison	Adobe Creative Cloud[13, 14]	Corel Draw[18]	Clo 3D and Clo 5 [17,10]	TukaCAD[12]
Software Availability	Available online. Compatible with both Windows and Mac based systems to cater wide range of users.	For Windows platform and commonly used for graphic design and illustration. Released a version of CorelDRAW specifically designed for Mac operating systems.	Compatible with both Windows and Mac operating systems.	Primarily Windows based software.
Lice	Subscriptio	Offers	The	Subscriptio

nsing Terms and Conditions,	n-based model for licensing with different plans based on user requirements and choice of softwares.	perpetual licenses with volume licensing options for educational institutions.	licensing terms and conditions for CLO 3D and CLO 5 in educational institutions varies depending on the region and specific agreements with the software provider.	n-based model for Licensing.
User Interface	Provides a unified user interface across its various applications, allowing for seamless workflow integration. Benefit- User can	Offers a user-friendly interface with tools and features accessible through customizable workspaces.	CLO 3D and CLO 5: CLO 3D and CLO 5 provide intuitive interfaces specifically designed for garment simulation and	TukaCAD offers a user-friendly interface with tools tailored for pattern making and garment design.

	access different softwares without the hassle to get used different user interface.		customization.	
Training Facilities	Offers extensive online resources, tutorials, and training materials, including Adobe Creative Cloud for Education program. Offerings: - • Adobe Authorized Training Centers • Onl	Provides online tutorials, training videos, and documentation to support users in learning the software. Offerings:- • Corel has authorized training partners in India that offer instructor-led training programs	Special Training to facility for educators and support staff mambers. • Consultation facility availability to effectively design a curriculum integrating CLO as a CAD software.	TukaCAD provides training and support resources, including online tutorials and documentation. Offerings:- • On-Site Training • Online Training • Tukatech organizes

	ine Training Resources • Adobe Education Exchange- An online community and platform for educators to connect, learn, and share resources. It offers a variety of professional development courses, workshops, and webinars • Adobe Certified Professional (ACP)	for CorelDRAW software. • Corel provides a range of online training resources, including video tutorials, webinars, and user guides, on their official website. • The CorelDRAW Community is an online platform where users, including educators, can connect, learn, and share their knowledge. It offers	• Online tutorials for further assistance and updates regarding software features and uses. • Online help center with manuals, tutorials, and FAQ's. • Online Design Community for experience sharing. • Newsroom- Regular posts, blogs for	training workshops and seminars, either at their own training centers or at industry events and conferences. • Comprehensive training documentation, user guides, manuals, and other educational resources that faculty members can refer to for self-study and continuous learning • Dedicated

	Program • The Adobe Education Community is an online platform where educators can access resources, participate in forums, and connect with other educators worldwide.	forums, blogs, and a knowledge base where users can ask questions, share tips and tricks, and find solutions to their queries. • CorelDRAW User Groups: In some cities in India, there are CorelDRAW user groups or design communities that organize regular meetups and events.	regular feature update announcements.	support team via email, phone, or online chat to address questions.
Cost	Adobe	Corel offers	Approxim	TukaCAD

of Purchasing Licenses	offers special pricing and licensing options for educational institutions, including K-12 schools, colleges, and universities. These plans are designed to provide access to Adobe Creative Cloud applications at a discounted rate. The cost for Adobe Creative Cloud plans can range from approximat	special pricing and volume licensing options for educational institutions. These options allow educational institutions to purchase multiple licenses at a discounted rate. The cost for CorelDRAW licenses can range from approximately INR 10,000 to INR 30,000 per license, depending on the specific version and licensing	ate cost of CLO 3D and CLO 5 software for academic institutions in Indian Rupees (INR) could range from Rs. 2,00,000 to Rs.8,00,000	offers educational licenses at discounted prices for educational institutions. 19$ per month

	ely INR 20,000 to INR 50,000 per year, depending on the specific plan and number of licenses required.	options.		
	The costs mentioned here are approximate. It varies case to case depending upon number of licences required, softwares included (in case of packages), currency conversion rates (for foreign software providers), duration of license, region of purchase, special trainings to be provided as per agreement between provider and institution, etc.			

4. A comparative analysis of technical skill requirements versus training provided by educational institutions to students along with gap identification

This section comprises of a comparison of the technical skill requirements to operate Computer-Aided Design (CAD) within the fashion, textile, and apparel industry versus the training provided by educational institutions to students so that gaps can be identified and worked upon to create a better alignment between academic programs and industry requirements.

4.1. Industry expectations vs. education

The fashion, textile, and apparel industry demands a high level of CAD proficiency, including software expertise, pattern-making skills, 3D modeling capabilities, and knowledge of technical specifications. While educational institutions provide CAD training, there might be variations in the depth and breadth of coverage, and industry-specific requirements may not always be fully met.

Educational institutes provide knowledge software basics, pattern-making, elementary knowledge of 3D modeling, and textile design. Some institutions collaborate with industry professionals, conduct workshops, or facilitate internships to provide students with practical exposure to CAD usage in real-world settings.

Gap Identified: *Difference in specialisation requirement and supply for CAD Software: A gap in software knowledge and proficiency when students enter the industry has been identified.*

4.2. Software selection

Industry professionals often use specialized CAD software tailored to fashion and textile design, such as Lectra or Gerber. However, educational institutions may primarily focus on teaching generic CAD software like Adobe Illustrator, which may not fully align with industry preferences.

Gap Identified: *Industry expectations may demand a higher level of proficiency.*

4.3. 3D modeling and visualization

The adoption of 3D technology is increasing in the industry. While some educational institutions provide training in 3D modeling, the extent of coverage and exposure to specialized 3D CAD software used in the industry may vary.

Gap Identified: *Students may not receive comprehensive training in 3D modeling and visualization, which could be a gap when working with industry-standard tools.*

4.4. Industry collaboration

Educational institutions collaborating with industry professionals or facilitating internships provide valuable exposure to industry practices. However, the level of collaboration may differ across institutions, impacting the degree of industry relevance in the training.

Gap Identified: *The extent of collaboration and exposure could result in a gap between academic training and the practical application of CAD skills in real-world industry settings.*

4.5. Continuous learning

The fashion, textile, and apparel industry is constantly evolving, with new CAD tools and techniques emerging. Professionals need to engage in continuous learning and stay updated with industry trends. Educational institutions should emphasize the importance of lifelong learning and encourage students to keep updating their CAD skills beyond their formal education.

Gaps Identified: *Lack of opportunities for students to update their CAD skills may result in lack of knowledge, lower* *employability which will ultimately result in failure in securing their position in the industry.*

4.6. Industry-specific CAD features

The fashion, textile, and apparel industry often require CAD software with industry-specific features. These may include fabric simulation, virtual prototyping, marker-making, color management, or integration with other design and production tools. The training provided by educational institutions should address these specific requirements to prepare students for industry expectations.

Gap Identified: *Academic programs may not fully address these features, leaving students less prepared to utilize them in real-world scenarios.*

4.7. Workflow integration

CAD skills in the industry involve integrating with other processes and departments, such as collaborating with pattern makers, sample makers, or production teams. Understanding the end-to-end workflow and the role of CAD within it is crucial. Institutions should provide insights into industry practices and encourage interdisciplinary collaboration to develop well-rounded professionals.

4.8. Soft skills and communication

While technical CAD skills are crucial, professionals in the industry also need strong communication, presentation, and collaboration skills. Educational institutions should focus on developing these soft skills alongside technical training to enhance students' ability to effectively communicate their CAD designs and collaborate with teams.

Gaps identified: *Industry professionals are required to understand the workflow and integrate with other departments effectively. Academic programs currently focus less on developing these soft skills and providing insights into industry practices to bridge this gap.*

5. Proposed measures to bridge gaps between industry and educational institutions

5.1. Curriculum enhancement

Educational institutions can review and enhance their curriculum to include industry-specific CAD software used in fashion, textile, and apparel design, such as Lectra or Gerber. Incorporating specialized software training can better prepare students for industry demands. This can be integrated in the form of an elective course for students.

5.2. Industry collaboration and internships

Institutions can establish stronger ties with industry professionals, companies, and organizations to facilitate collaboration opportunities, guest lectures, workshops, and internships. This exposure can provide students with real-world insights, practical experience, and a better understanding of industry expectation and also help them decide their targets.

5.3. Continuous professional development

Emphasize the importance of continuous learning and professional development beyond formal education. Encourage students to participate in workshops, webinars, industry conferences, and online courses to stay updated with the latest CAD tools, techniques, and industry trends.

5.4. Integration of 3D technology

Given the growing adoption of 3D modeling and visualization in the industry, educational institutions should incorporate specialized 3D CAD software training and techniques into their curriculum. This integration can better equip students with the skills needed to excel in areas like virtual prototyping and 3D garment simulation.

5.5. Industry-relevant projects

Incorporate industry-relevant projects into the curriculum to provide students with hands-on experience in working on real-world CAD design challenges. Collaborate with industry partners to identify project opportunities that align with current industry needs and trends.

5.6. Soft skills development

Recognize the importance of soft skills, such as communication, collaboration, and presentation abilities, alongside technical CAD skills. Include modules or workshops that focus on developing these skills to enhance students' overall professional readiness.

5.7. Industry feedback mechanism

Establish a structured feedback mechanism with industry professionals, alumni, and employers to gather insights into the skill gaps and emerging industry requirements. Regularly update the curriculum based on this feedback to ensure it remains relevant and aligned with industry expectations.

5.8. Faculty development and industry exposure

Provide opportunities for faculty members to enhance their knowledge and skills through industry training programs, workshops, or internships. Encourage faculty members to maintain active connections with the industry to stay updated with the latest trends and practices, which can be incorporated into the teaching process.

5.9. Research and innovation

Encourage research initiatives focused on CAD technology, its applications in the industry, and emerging trends. Promote collaboration between academia and industry to explore innovative solutions and stay at the forefront of technological advancements.

5.10. Industry standards and regulations

The fashion, textile, and apparel industry adhere to certain standards and regulations related to sizing, fit, safety, and sustainability. CAD professionals should be familiar with these standards and incorporate them into their designs. Institutions can incorporate relevant industry standards and regulations into their curriculum to prepare students for compliance requirements.

By implementing these measures, educational institutions can bridge the gaps between industry expectations and academic offerings, ensuring that students are better equipped with the technical skills and industry-relevant knowledge needed to succeed in CAD tasks within the fashion, textile, and apparel industry.

6. Conclusions

As per the need of current technology era, every industry has to incorporate technology to maximum possible extent to enhance efficiency and productivity, standardization, maintain a balance between demand and supply while still being profitable, putting their best foot front to establish an identity and reputation. Technology provides automation and time efficiency so that resources can be directed towards ensuring the use to human creativity and intellect towards innovation, growth and development. Fashion, Apparel and Textile Industry has adopted technology in each and every aspect of work as discussed in detailed through this chapter. As industrial needs for skill supply are largely met be educational institutions, curriculum must be adapted to industry needs and current work culture to ensure employability of their students. To effectively utilize CAD software in the fashion education curriculum, students need to acquire essential skills to operate these sophisticated tools. Proficiency in digital design, patternmaking, 3D visualization, and technical specification generation are fundamental skills that aspiring fashion professionals must develop. Apart from full feature CAD softwares, various mobile applications are available for Android and IOS which can also be included in curriculum as an elementary step for students towards CAD. By incorporating CAD software into their curriculum, educational institutions can empower students with practical skills that align with industry standards and enhance their employability. Current gaps must be addressed to improve the alignment between academic programs and industry requirements.

References

1. Abhishek, Ashish, Jain, Siddhant. "What Are the Design Software That Are Taught in NIFT and FDDI?" *Quora*, www.quora.com/What-are-the-design-software-that-are-taught-in-NIFT-and-FDDI.

2. http://www.astortechnologies.com/products-1

3. http://www.jacqcad.com/index.html
4. https://audaces.com/en/blog/what-is-cad-software-and-why-use-it-to-produce-fashion
5. https://geminicad.com/
6. https://in.apparelresources.com/technology-news/manufacturing-tech/10-popular-cad-solution-providers/
7. https://lectra.com/en/products/gerber-accumark-accunest-fashion
8. https://nqr.gov.in/sites/default/files/annex1Curriculum_SOFTWARE%20APPLICATION%20IN%20FASHION%20DESIGN.pdf
9. https://optitex.com/
10. https://support.clo3d.com/hc/en-us/articles/115000307168-CLO-system-requirements-July-2020-?page=2#!
11. https://textilelearner.net/computer-aided-fashion-designing/
12. https://tukatech.com/tukacad/
13. https://www.adobe.com/in/creativecloud.html
14. https://www.adobe.com/in/offer-terms/cc_full_special_offer.html?promoid=55KD8QMC&mv=other
15. https://www.aryabharathipolytechnic.ac.in/syllabus/appareldesign&fabr.techlgy/sixthsem/CAD.pdf
16. https://www.cdesignfashion.com/en/fashion-plm-product-lifecycle-management/
17. https://www.clo3d.com/en/enterprise/academic
18. https://www.coreldraw.com/en/

19. https://www.dsifd.com/courses/fashion-cad-colleges-institutes.php
20. https://www.lectra.com/en/products/modaris-expert
21. https://www.morgantecnica.com/
22. https://www.patternsmith.com/
23. https://www.texintel.com/software/digifab
24. https://www.textronic.com/
25. https://www.textronic.com/cad-systems.html
26. https://www.textronic.com/design-3D.html
27. https://www.ventureradar.com/organisation/Textile%20Vision/79765c4f-5afc-4bae-b0dc-6dd0290fd365
28. Kaur, Prabhjot. (2011). CAD/CAM TECHNOLOGY: A BOON TO APPAREL INDUSTRY. Gyan Management. 5. 157-168.

9.

MICROFIBERS: PRODUCTION TECHNIQUES, PROPERTIES & USES

Dr. Beenu Singh and Dr. Manisha Gahlot

G. B. Pant University of Agriculture and Technology, Pantnagar Uttarakhand

Email:

Abstract

Microfiber is defined as a fibre with linear density of not more than 1 decitex or less and greater than 0.3 decitex, including staple fibers and filaments. They even produce fibers with a thickness of 0.3 decitex, which is often referred to as super microfibers. Currently available microfibers differ, mainly in terms of their size, from standard fibers but also have a lower degree of property difference compared to ordinary fibers.

1. Introduction

Japanese introduced the first "micro-denier" products during 1970s. Then followed the developments in Europe during the 1980s, and since the 1990s American fiber manufacturers have been following suit. Currently, the production of microfibers is mainly carried out in polyester and nylon. Ultramicrofiber technology was already in place as soon as microfibers were invented. These fibers are in the range of less than 0.3decitex and, to a great extent, upto 0.1decitex. The production of such fibers can take place in a variety of ways, entailing the decomposition of large fibers into numerous smaller ones. The relationship of linear fiber density and classification is shown in Table 1.

Table 1: Linear fiber density of microfibers and its classification

Fiber count, decitex/f	Fiber classification
Greater than 7.0	Coarse
7.0 to 2.4	Medium fine
2.4 to 1.0	Fine
1.0 to 0.3	Micro
Less than 0.3	Super-microfibers (range of nm that is less than 0.1 decitex)

2. Trade names of microfibers

1. Trivera Finess (Polyester) (Trivera Interactive, U.S.A.)
2. Fortel Microspun (Polyester) (U.K)
3. Shingosen (Polyester) (Japan)
4. Tactle Micro (Nylon)
5. Silky touch (Nylon)
6. Micro-supreme (Acrylic)

3. Manufacturing of microfibers

In general, fibers of linear density below 1.0 decitex are regarded as microfibers. Although the microfiber technology has been available for a long time, it was not until the 1980s that this type of fibre began to attract significant demand. Presently available microfibers differ, mainly in their size, from average fibers but also have a very low molecular weight difference compared as to standard fibers. Microfibers were first introduced by Toray company in the world then followed by Teijin, ICI, Hoechst, DuPont and some others.

Compared to silk, which is up to thirty times the fineness of cotton, 40 times the fineness of wool and 100 times that of human hair, as shown in Figure 1, microfibers are ten times thinner. Generally, fiber producer use such term as: greater than 7.0 decitex for coarse fibers; 7.0 to 2.4 decitex for medium fine to normal fibers; 2.4 to 1.0 decitex for fine fibers; 1.0 to 0.3 decitex for microfibers; and less than 0.3 decitex for super, ultrafine microfibers.

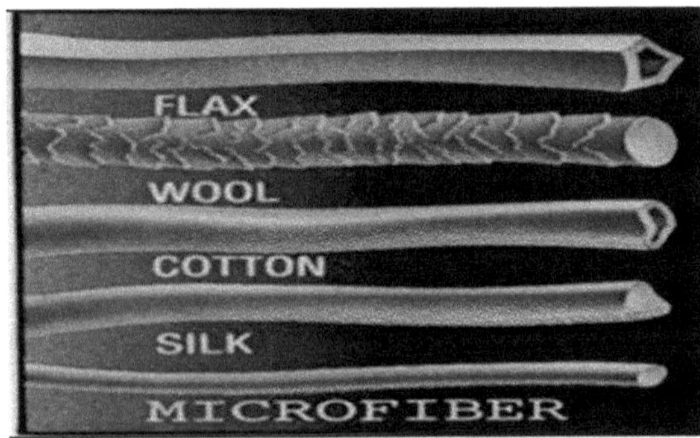

Figure1: Comparison of fineness of different textile fibers

Microfibers are extruded using more expensive and complex technologies than traditional one. Because they are delicate yarns, microfibers must be handled with extreme care in textile mill operations. Microfibers can be formed using a variety of techniques, such as modified conventional spinning. Microfibers can be produced using any of the three traditional spinning techniques, including melt spinning, wet spinning, and dry spinning.

Conditions for polymerization, spinning, and drawing must be carefully chosen for this process. This process can be used to create microfibers made of polyester, nylon, and acrylic. The extrusion spinnerets should have very small holes, each of which should be able to produce a continuous filament despite complicated temperature and rheological variations.

3.1 Chips and their quality used to make microfibers

- Consistency in polymer composition: Composition should free from foreign matter
- Narrow molecular weight distribution: Chain length between monomers should be short so that it affects the molecular weight of polymer. Low molecular weight monomers should be used
- Viscosity should be kept consistent
- Smooth and tailless polymer chips
- Chips need to be identical in shape and size
- Off quality chips should be avoided
- Chips of best quality available
- The drying procedure should be as consistent as feasible, and the residence period for the chips should be uniform
- During the molten stage, the dried chips' moisture recovery rate should be less than 0.005% to avoid

hydrolytic deterioration. Hence, for the hassle-free manufacture of microfibers, the precise moisture content in the dried chips must be specified. Therefore, continuous drying is preferred over batch drying method.

4. Manufacturing methods of microfibers

4.1. Continuous filament type

4.1.1. Direct spinning

Direct spinning is a conventional spinning method, in which spinning conditions are optimized to produce ultra fine fibers. Following are the problems faced in the application of conventional melt spinning method:

1. Breakdown of fiber
2. Filament thickness variation
3. Clogging of spinneret
4. Variability in denier among filaments of a single yarn

4.1.1.1. Moriki technique

Multicomponent fibers are not produced by Moriki process from a single spinneret. Each core stream is fed using tubes, however their number is constrained by the smallest particle size, necessitating a large amount of space. Very fine tubes makes expensive method for their collection on retainer plate. While cleaning parts of spin pack, it is hard to avoid damage of tubes. It also becomes difficult to clean each tube from inside. Moriki device when it is clean and undamaged can be used to manufacture very uniform high-quality fibers.

4.1.1.2. Kessler echnique

There is one central stream and around its periphery many polymer side streams are placed in machine inserts. Due to limitation in size of side tubes makes this technique only suitable for spinning a limited number of composite filaments per spinneret. Cleaning of spinneret is a very tedious work because for a single spinneret with one thousand or more inserts. This technique is quite suitable for making filament yarn of continuous length.

4.1.1.3. Sheath core spinning method

This technique involves melting and mix-annealing of two distinct polymers that have been combined. Conjugate fiber consists of a concentric circular sheath around a core. This sheath is removed away to create the ultra-fine fibers.

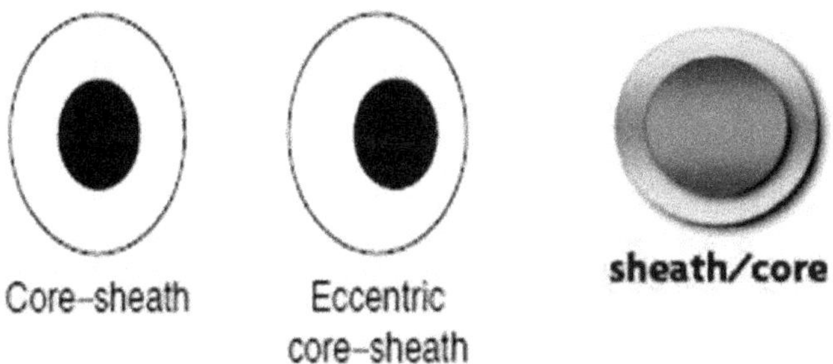

Figure 2: Cross section of Sheath Core Type Fibers

4.1.1.4. Super drawing technique

There's no molecular orientation involved in this technique. It is possible to produce staple fibers with a continuous density below 0.5 decitex at the highest drawing ratios. The principle of this technique is that the yarn can be stretched to 10 to 75 times more as compared to their conventional draw ratios i.e. 3 to 6 times more. But the condition is that the drawing should be carried out at drawing conditions at minimum crystallizing temperature and the type of heating the fiber including the temperature range.

4.1.2. Indirect/conjugate spinning

The conjugate spinning is used to produce ultra fine fibers which are uniform. This method of spinning was developed to solve technical problems occurring in direct spinning. Okamoto *et. al.* (Toray) and Matsui *et. al.* (Kanebo) modified the spinneret structure for the extrusion of conjugate fibers of highly dispersed conjugate components. Innovations are taking place in bi-component spinning of yarns, In this spinning process, the island in sea type, split type and then multilayer type are major types of fibers produced.

4.1.2.1. Separation type

In this type, microfiber is obtained by physical or chemical treatment of bi-component filaments which contain two type of polymers and then dividing them into different types of filaments. The filament is easier to split into the segment than in the fabric. Suitable polymer combinations for splitting bi-component filaments are polyamides/polyester and polyester/polyolefins. The important points to be considered for selecting the polymer combinations are as follows:

- Incompatiblility
- Same melt viscosities at common extruder temperature;
- Weak adhesivity

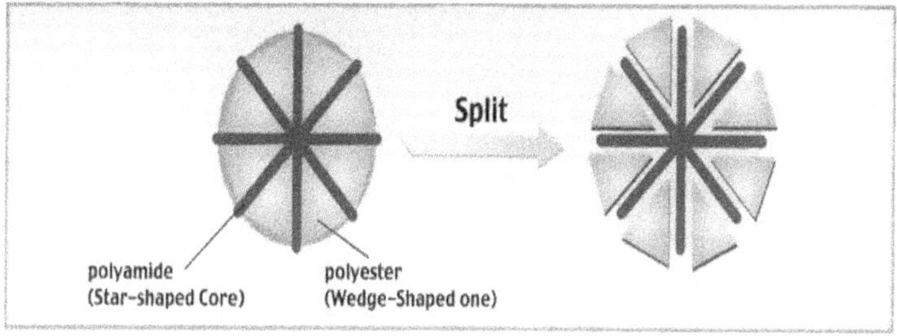

Figure 3: Cross section of Split type Microfiber

4.1.2.2. Dissolution technique

This type of microfiber is made of bicomponent fibers with different polymer types. Relatively thick bicomponent filaments having different incompatible polymers are spun into fabrics. During the chemical treatment of fabric with a solvent, one component dissolves and is removed, leaving the other component as microfiber. Polyester and nylon microfibers are produced using this method. For commercial production 20:80 ratio of soluble or insoluble polymers has been used to produce bi-component filaments as fine as 2 decitex and a final dissolved filament with a linear density of about 0.50 decitex.

The important key points for selecting the polymer combinations are as follows:

- Solubility should be high
- Stability of polymer at the time of extrusion
- At extrusion temperature the properties of polymers should be compatible
- Recoverable nature of polymer
- Polymer should not be toxic, polluting, corrosive

The different combinations used for soluble and insoluble polymers are polystyrene-polyamide and polystyrene-polyester to form fibers successfully.

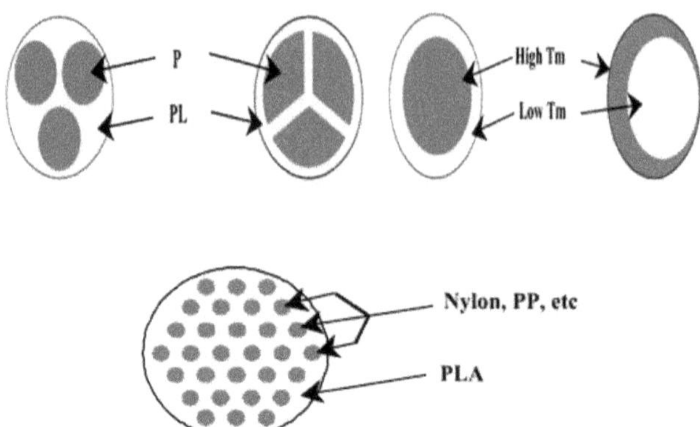

Figure 4: Cross section of Dissolved type Microfiber

4.1.2.3. Island in sea type

In this method removal of sea component is done by dissolving it in a solvent. Two component polymer is extruded from spinneret which is conjugate type or sheath-core type.

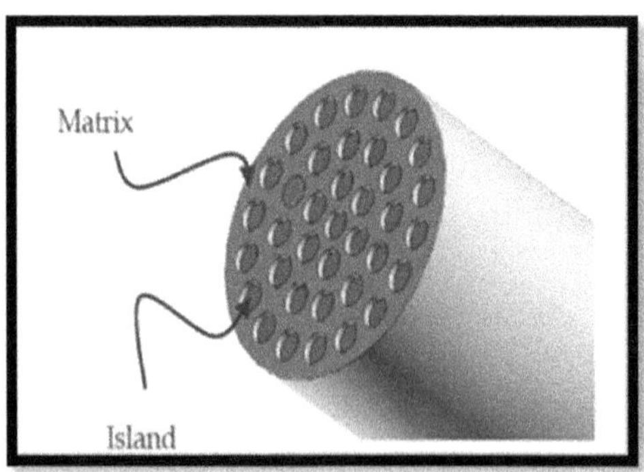

Figure 5: Cross sectional view of Island in sea type microfibers

Polyester, polypropylene, nylon, polyethylene, polyphenylene sulfide are used as island components. Mostly used Sea components are polystyrene, copolymer of 2-ethylhexyl acrylate or ethylene terephthalate copolymer and sodium sulfo-isophthalate and these are removed by dissolving in solvent.

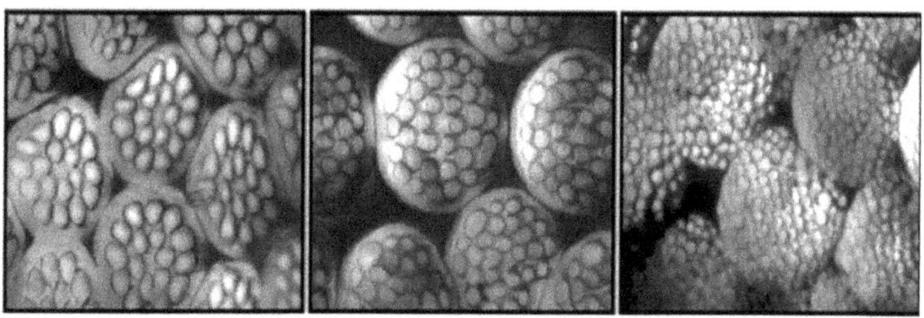

Fig.6: Cross sectional view of Bi-component fibers: 18 islands, 36 islands and 108 islands

4.1.2.4. Multilayer type

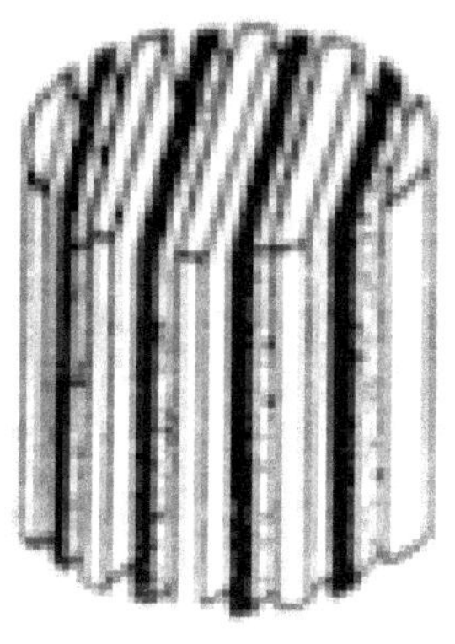

Liquid can be multi layered form have been applied to multilayer type spinning for which static mixtures are used. Kuraray, Kanebo and Toray are Japanese companies first investigated multilayer type spinning technology. Two components which are spun into a conjugate fiber i.e. polyester and nylon 6 are of multilayered structure. Their cross section is oval shaped. During the dyeing process, they are micro fiberized into filaments of 0.2-0.3 denier.

4.2. Random staple type

4.2.1. Melt blown or jet spinning

The melt of polymer is blown apart with an stream of air jet immediately after extrusion, that is why it is also known as jet spinning. In this method application of a spraying technique is more rather than actual spinning.

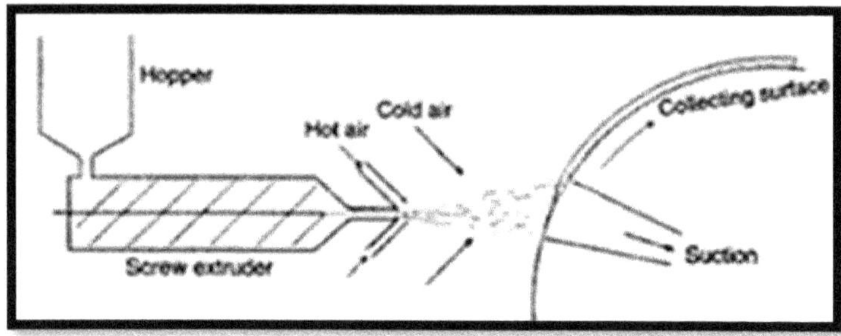

Figure 7: Schematic View of Melt Blown Process

Suitable range of melt viscosity of fibers is required to get the required results. It should be lower than that of the conventional polypropylene used for melt spinning The spinneret has a sharp edge and jet streams blows off the extruded polymer melt into ultra fine fibers.

4.2.2. Flash spinning

Flash spun fibers is known as ultra fine fibers. Network of fibers is obtained by spreading a single stream of fibers which is spun from single spinneret hole. The filament thickness varies from 0.01 denier per filament in the range of 0.1 - 0.15 denier. The cross-section of filament is not circular and some filaments also have microbubbles. Homogeneous solutions are formed at high temperature and under high pressure by dissolving polymer.

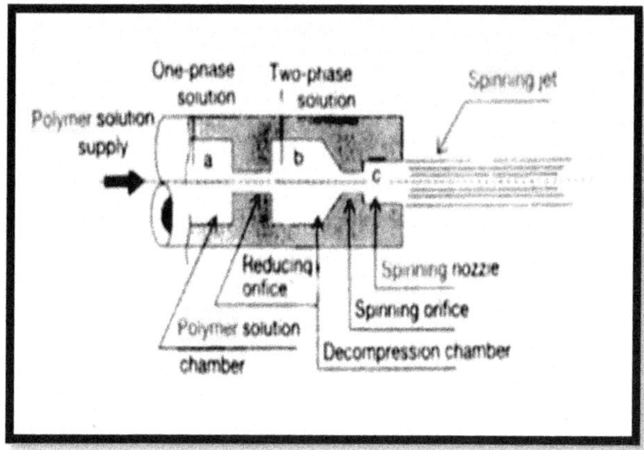

Figure 8: Flash Spinning Process

A turbid solution is formed when spinning solution is separated in liquid phase. It is jetted out througha nozzle into air to form a network of fibers and known as plexifilament. Polyethylene is dissolved in hydrocarbon or methylene is used to form micro-networked fibers. Ethylene chloride and flurocarbon were used as solvents. This technology was firstly aimed to produce synthetic paper but nowadays it is used to produce wrapping material. Due to high spinning speed it is difficult to form fiber, so the product is made into sheet.

4.2.3. Polymer blend spinning

Two components are mixed by extruding and drawing a polymer melt and conjugated fibers are obtained. Melt viscosities and mixing ratio determine the arrangement of dispersed and non-dispersed components. By removing matrix component microfibers were obtained. Fiber fineness cannot be controlled and fiber often breaks during spinning. Spin ability depends on combination of polymers. Dispersed polymer phase is drawn to yield microfibers.

4.2.4. Centrifugal spinning

Centrifugal spinning is an alternative method for producing microfibers at high speed and low cost. The spinning fluid is placed in a rotating spinning head. The rotating speed reaches a critical value, the centrifugal force overcomes the surface tension of the spinning fluid to eject a liquid jet from the nozzle tip of the spinning head. Jet undergoes a stretching process, eventually deposited on the collector, forming solidified microfibers. The technique is simple and enables the rapid fabrication of microfibers for various applications.

4.2.5. Fibrillation

In this technique fibrillation by beating a fiber or film. Turbulent flow for coagulation of polymer solution is also used for fibrillation.

4.2.6. Burst spinning

Ultra fine staple fibers are formed through bursting. Blowing agent or gas is used for bursting the polymer.

5. Processing of microfibers

5.1. Carding

It is impossible to card microfibers at a production rate as compared to conventional fiber types. Thus, the cost per unit mass of production increases. When carding, a higher density of carding thread points is required.

5.2. Winding and warping

All guide surfaces must be very smooth and in top mechanical condition, as microfibers are likely to break more easily than regular filament.

5.3. Sizing

Microfiber warp sizing should preferably done with single-end tying machines to minimize filament breakage at split rods. If a single finish size is not available, a pre-dryer is required. Microfiber yarn has a larger selection of sizes and is also more wanted.

5.4. Weaving

In general, tensions should be kept as low as possible. Weft yarn in air jet or water jet looms requires some finish to work as efficiently.

5.5. Finishing on microfibers

Finishes which are applied on microfibers are:

- Charisma: suede like finish
- Ultima: water-repellent finish
- Moonstruck: silk like soft sueded finish,
- Micromist: brushed finish
- Regal: dry hand finish
- Silkmore: sandwashed silk finish
- Stanza: water repellent finish

6. Structure of microfibers

Some microfibers are waterproof "flat weave" used primarily in the textile industry, such as clothing and watch straps. "Flat weave" microfiber is not suitable for cleaning or polishing, as its absorbency is half that of "split weave" microfiber. "Split Weave" microfibers are made from polyamide fibers by splitting polyester fibers, which increases the surface area and in turn the amount of water that the cloth or mop can absorb. As the threads are divided, thousands of loops are formed per square inch. These loops are perfect for collecting small dust and dirt particles without rubbing surfaces.

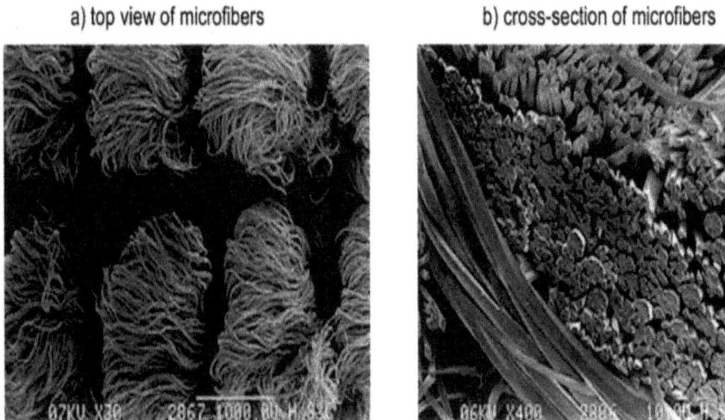

Figure 9: SEM of Microfiber fabric

6.1. Properties

- Linear density is ultra-fine which is less than 0.1 decitex/f, known to be finer than the most delicate silk
- Very good drapeability along with very soft fabric and luxurious hand similar to suede touch
- It can be washed and dry-cleaned
- Shrinkage resistant
- Very high strength
- Rain, wind, and cold insulation
- Anti-microbial in nature

- Hypoallergenic in nature so helpful to those suffering from allergies
- Non electrostatic
- Microfibers are super-absorbent material which absorbs 7 times of their weight in water
- Drying time is one-third times as compared to general fibers
- Environmental friendly in nature

6.2. Absorption

Microfibers have high density and large surface area, absorb up to 7 times their weight in water, which makes the synthetic material perfect for use in cloths and mops.

6.3. Hygienic

Microfibers attract and catch pathogens, bacteria and viruses until cleaned in the wash. Microfiber cloths and mops perfect for use in food preparation areas, dining areas, hospitals, and health care establishments, reducing the risk of illness and germs being spread around. The inorganic nature of microfiber fabric and mops is good for them to catch and destroy harmful bacteria as pathogens love to feed on organic material.

6.4. Non-abrasive

Non-abrasive, clothes, mops and pads do not have a negative effect on surfaces, leaving any waxing or finish undamaged. It is ideal for use on furniture and flooring. Microfiber fabrics are extremely durable, with thousands of 'loops' per square inch of material and up to 200,000 strands of fiber per square inch of material. It can withstand up to 500 washes, enabling you to reuse the man-made cleaning products time and time again.

6.5. Applications

Microfiber is widely used in these areas:

1. Industrial
2. Medical
3. Apparel use
4. Household applications
5. Sports
6. Construction

6.6. Industrial

Industry uses microfibers for cleaning up oil spills. Mats are formed from fibers and are placed over oil spills wherever absorption of oil is required. Another benefit is that it is low cost. In air pollution control process, rotatable collector is employed for removing airborne particulate matter.

6.7. Medical

Microfibers nonwovens are easier to use, more versatile, safer and easy to dispose. Therefore they are used for making surgical gowns, protective face masks, gloves, surgical packs, bedding and linens of patients.

6.8. Apparel use

Kuraray, manmade leather has introduced new Amaretta JP manmade suede, made up of polyester microfiber and polyurethane resin which is microporous in nature.

Unitika Ltd. has introduced stretchable synthetic suede, which is made from polyester micro fibers (82%) and a polyurethane resin (18%), effect similar to leather.

Kanebo Gohsen Ltd. has produced Beledano which uses Belima SX microfibers (0.05 denier), bi component spinning, split type, use to make apparel like coats and jackets. Used in making microfibers jackets, 100% polyester sueded microfibers and water repellent finish.

6.9. Household applications

Superabsorbent towels, eliminates use of soaps and detergents Microfibers have large surface area to grab grease and dirt. Synthetic yarns such as polyester or nylon-polyester mixture of 0.2 to 0.3 denier are used. Microfibers are widely used as wiping clothes for cleaning utensils of kitchen/household furnishings/cars/mirror of windows/bath towels/face cloths/cleaning of eye glass/face cloths/mittens.

6.10. Sports

Hand sewn football made of solid polyurethane, four layers of microfiber textile, one layer of french foam of neoprene and natural latex with butyl valve.

6.11. Microfibers for cleaning

Microfiber products are appropriate for clean-up many things. Microfibers "scrape" the dirt, mark of stain from the surface and retain the dirt particles in the fabric itself until it is washed. While clothes used for regular cleaning, move the dirt and dust particles from one area to another. The method for cleaning dirt with ordinary fibers and microfibers is shown in the Figure 10.

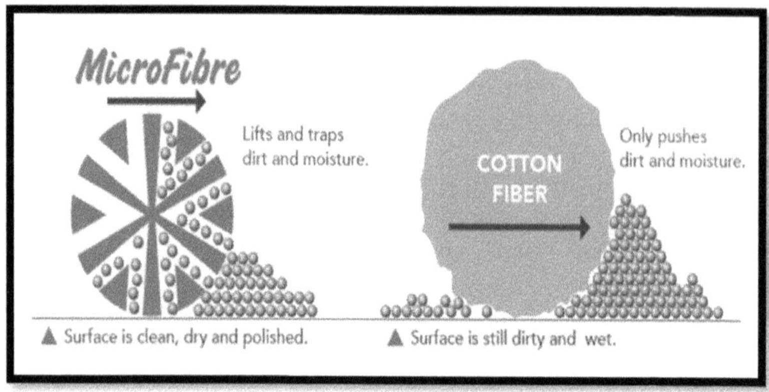

Figure 10: Cleaning action of microfibers

Microfiber is well suited for professional groomers, and car dealers. They are good for people suffering from asthma and allergies. They remove dust and dust mites better without using chemicals. Fingerprints are removed from surface with the help of microfibers. They change the static charge of the surface, which is important for cleaning screens of TV, monitors of computer and mirror.

6.12. Construction

Microfibers are used for making composites. It is multilayer material which consists of different layers having different property in each layer. The different multilayer materials used for construction possess different properties. Polypropylene and bicomponent microfibers are two important components which act as a binder fiber between to hold the different layers.

- Concrete reinforced with microfibers (to strengthen and prevent cracks)

- Insulation material, used as a multi-functional liquid transport media namely two layers acquisition and distribution
- Microfiber woven fabrics is used for laminated products i.e. lamination between textile material and boards and for dimensional stability.
- Polypropylene and bicomponent (PP/PE) microfibers can improve the structural performance and functionality of composite materials.
- Microfiber enable light weight structures in composites (PP fibers have the lowest specific weight of all fibers)

7. Miscellaneous

7.1. High performance filter fabrics

- Excellent filtration, because of fine compact structure
- Used in air and fluid filtration both
- It provide permanent polarization to the non-woven

7.2. Imitation leather

- Firstly produced by Japan commercially. Nonwoven was impregnated to and was produced from PET, PA, PAN microfibers with PU.
- It has advantages of uniformity, ease of care, dimensional stability. Improved absorbent products based on microfiber technology were introduced by using pressure sensitive microfibers
- Widely used for sanitary napkins, garments used for incontinence, and disposable diapers.
- Used in microfiber pile fabric by utilizing MicroSupreme (high tech acrylic) such as

Microfabric, MicroLana and GlenPile micro pile fabrics. These are used in hightech fashion accessories like branded coat and sportswear accessories like gloves, hays, scarves, robes, footwear, and loungewear, home textiles.

- Composite fibers have fineness in range 0.0001 – 0.5 denier and core to sheath weight ratio range of 10:90-70:30.
- Imitation leather can be combined with elastic material (such as polyurethane) to produce artificial leather like sued which have excellent softness, touch, feel and colour fastness.

8. Conclusions

Microfiber is a new generation fiber of very fine man-made yarns. There are still many unexplored possibilities in the field of design, processing, production, and usage of microfiber. Along with commercial raw materials, PAC, and PES, PA other raw material in the future will also be included in special selection such as cellulose.

References

1. https://books.google.co.in/books?id=J23dVdRp72cC&pg=PA130&dq=fibrillation+or+violent+flexing&hl=en&sa=X&ved=0ahUKEwiL9aiyg
2. https://books.google.co.in/books?id=sxUsqJQUKY0C&pg=PA203&lpg=PA203&dq=fukushima+et+al+polymer+blend+spinning&source
3. http://textilelearner.blogspot.in/2012/01/microfibers-properties-of-microfibers.html
4. http://autexrj.com/cms/zalaczone_pliki/1-07-3.pdf

5. http://nopr.niscair.res.in/bitstream/123456789/22858/1/IJFTR%2027(3)%20307-314.pdf

10.

INSTAGRAM: A NEW-AGE TOOL FOR PROMOTING MICRO APPAREL AND HOME LINEN BUSINESS

Dr. Pooja Gaba Adlakha[1] and Dr. Seema Chawla[2]

[1]Creative Head, Craftales, New Delhi

[2]Assistant Professor, Krishi Vigyan Kendra. Sri Ganganagar (Swami Keshwanand Rajasthan Agricultural University), Rajasthan.

Email: drpoojagaba19@gmail.com

ABSTRACT

In the era of smartphones, 85 percent of the global population has a smartphone and a smartphone has an operating system, web browsing, and the ability to run software applications. Instagram is one such application that allows you to upload free photos and videos free of cost. It also allows editing and geographical tagging and is available in 31 languages across the globe.

Earlier, anyone who wanted to sell apparel on a small scale had to own a shop but now with the help of Instagram, many budding entrepreneurs have followed their passion and have scaled up their businesses. Apart from new brands, many established and major brands such as Nike, Gucci, Burberry, and Zara Home have their Instagram pages, and millions of people follow them to know about the latest updates.

The chapter will highlight a few brands that started their journey from their homes and gradually scaled up and have clientele across the globe. They have not only fulfilled their dreams but have also generated employment for the artisans, tailors, and logistics industry.

Keywords: *BRAND, APPARELS, ARTISANS, HOME LINENS*

1. Introduction

Instagram is a free photo and video-sharing application available on iPhone and Android. The application was released in October 2010 and was acquired by Facebook in 2012. The major advantage of Instagram is that it can be freely shared by users. Many people have the desire to start their business but due to heavy rentals and staff salaries, people were not starting off their venture. Instagram has been a boom for such aspiring small businessmen/ women. Nowadays many Apparel and Home linen brands have made their mark in the textile and apparel industry by offering the product at the doorstep of the customers. The Instagram account owner creates an account and regularly showcases product photos and videos for the target customers. Several hashtags are also used to enhance the reach of the post.

Many brand owners take the help of digital marketing to promote their products to enhance sales. Digital marketing is considered the most suitable way to promote brands or services through social media in a more organized manner. Let us understand what Digital marketing is. Any marketing that uses electronic devices can be used by marketing specialists to promote the product via online videos, display advertisements, search engine marketing, paid social advertisements, and social media posts.

Digital marketing is also called online marketing in order to promote the brands to connect with potential customers using the Internet and other forms of digital communication. Instagram is being used by several brands for their businesses and is used for brand awareness, boosting sales, and building and tracking audience engagement with the brand. A promotional strategy is used on Instagram by adding money to its account and it runs the post selected to the target audience. Instagram helps a company to elevate in myriad ways, including

- Engagement
- Increasing website traffic
- Branding
- Content Creation
- Advertising
- Building trust
- Sharing announcements and updates
- Customer connection
- Gathering feedback
- Showing off creativity.
- New launches
- Regular Interaction with the customer

- Feedback

In this paper, based on my research and my experience of running Craftales as a brand I would be covering a few brands who have scaled in the past few years and have launched their websites / offline stores after starting their brands on Instagram. A few brands that started selling their products through Instagram and have scaled up well are as follows:

- The Indian Ethnic Company, Mumbai
- Hathkargha, Dehradun
- House of Chikankari, Delhi
- Fabriclore, Jaipur
- Bed and Beyond, Jhansi
- Tints and Textures, New Delhi

2. Apparel:

2.1. The Indian ethnic company

The start-up started in 2016 with an investment of 50,000 rupees where one of the founders bought 50 meters of Ajrakh fabric and within a span of 7 years the turnover of the company has reached 15 crores. The brand started from Hetal and Lekhinee's Mumbai home where a nearby tailor was approached to stitch the designed Kurtis. The founders shared that they got the first orders from Goa and Kerala through their Facebook Page. The brand promotes sustainable fashion; the fabrics used are made out of natural dyes and the promotion of the apparel is done through dance visuals majorly. At present the brand operates through its Instagram and Facebook page, website, and three offline stores in Mumbai with 25 employees and is associated with more than 100 artisans. The Indian Ethnic company has managed to dress over 3000 people living in over 450 cities and 19 countries so far.

2.2. Hathkargha

Hathkargha is another clothing brand that sells unstitched suit sets, sarees, stitched blouses, and Home Linens. The brand started its operations around six years ago by participating in exhibitions. The founder shares the new collection by wearing them and promotes it through its Instagram page to its followers.

The brand operates through its offline store located in Dehradun, Uttrakhand, and has 3.5 lakh followers on its Instagram page. Every new collection is informed through videos/ photos to its followers on its Instagram page and is uploaded on the website for sale. Majorly, the brand sells Cotton, Chanderi, and Mulmul fabric in her collection. Block Printing, tassel attachment, and machine embroidery can also be seen on a few pieces. A brand that has grown up through participation in exhibitions showcases its products regularly through its social media page and has collections from several states of India.

2.3. House of chikankari

House of Chikankari was started by a mother-daughter duo in November 2020 with the woman Chikankari Kurtas. One of the Founders started sharing their visuals on their Instagram page 'House of Chikankari' by wearing the kurtas out for sale. The mother-daughter duo made good headway in popularising the brand, closing the first year with a revenue of 33 lakhs. The hand embroidery work is done by women artisans in Lucknow and now employs more than 5000 women. The garments are stitched by third-party manufacturers in Lucknow. The brand launched its website within six months of its launch and caters to formal and casual wear kurtas, suit sets, and tops in all fabric types for different seasons. The women's apparel is priced from Rs. 2000 to Rs. 13,000 and is available in all sizes. In February 2023 the brand raised 75 lakhs in equity of 3.75% from India's popular TV show Shark Tank India. House of Chikankari has become a global brand within a span of fewer than three years.

3. Fabrics

3.1. Fabriclore

Fabriclore is a Jaipur-based online retailer for running fabrics. It was founded in 2016 by three friends who started posting the fabric shoots on their Instagram and Facebook Pages. An online brand that aims to revive India's traditional and modern fabrics by delivering high-quality curated fabrics.

Fabriclore has created a team of designers par global standards which is abreast with modern design pedigree and high-quality equipment support. Recently, the brand has also built a walk-in studio where one can explore 300-plus certified fabrics from global suppliers. Fabriclore also creates fabrics on demand in 21 days and delivers materials to major retailers such as Lifestyle, Reliance Trends, Iconic, Tatacliq, and Azaadi.

The whole idea of Fabriclore started when one of the founder's fathers had a fabric shop in Jaipur city and he started posting images of the fabrics on his newly made Instagram page and got his first order in the first week of posting. With regular updates of various fabrics, content, designs, creative draping of the fabrics, and with wonderful logistics the brand has grown up well. Fabriclore has around 100 employees and it has become a known brand for fabric lovers.

3.2. Home linens: bed and beyond

It started around three years ago in the year 2020 and sells Home Linens. The brand started with just one piece in each design for the bedsheets to be sold and now they keep 100 pieces per design as an inventory before the launch of a new design—another Homegrown brand that started in a small town in Jhansi, known for Rani Laxmi Bai. The power of high-speed internet and social media coverage has promoted so many women to start their ventures to fulfill their desired dreams and to empower themselves and the people around them. The brand owner sells Quilts, Bedsheets, Pouches, and Quilted Bed Covers, majorly made from the Block Printing technique which supports the local artisans involved in the Dyeing and Printing industry of Jaipur, Rajasthan.

3.3. Tints and textures

It is also another home-grown home linen brand based out of Delhi which is also promoting Home linens through its Instagram page. This brand owner also sells Quilts, Bedsheets, Pouches, and Quilted Bedcovers which are handcrafted. The scrolling history of posts reveals that constant posting about the product photos and videos has increased the queries regarding the product, its sale, and as well as its followers.

4. Some advantages of shopping from small businesses

1. The goods are locally made in smaller quantities which results in better quality products that also tend to be ethical and sustainable.
2. The products made locally involve local craftspeople and hence employ people who are needy and have good knowledge of the craft.
3. It engages employment within the community or region.
4. The consumer connects well with the brand, the people involved, and the vision of the brand. Instagram added a “support small businesses” sticker feature for their stories which has been seeing a huge rise. Choosing more home-grown brands over the high street is a conscious decision. We must make and improve our consumption habits.

5. Challenges faced by new fashion/ home small business owners

1. Building brand.
2. Intense competition
3. Financial limitation
4. Production challenges due to small quantities
5. Less space and Inventory management
6. Seasonal product demand
7. Changing trends

8. Earning customer loyalty.
9. Ethical consideration in product and labor
10. Finding Investors and Raising Funds

6. Conclusions

The digital era has transformed the lives of many people and the Internet and social media have helped many brands and services to reach the unreached. The availability of raw materials, cheap labor costs and excellent logistics across India and internationally, and cheap access to the Internet have enabled small business owners to launch, promote and sell their products nationally and Internationally.

House of Chikankari, The Indian Ethnic Co., and Fabriclore have shown a way to many people who want to start their venture but are short of capital. With merely an investment of 50,000 to 3,00,000 lakhs these brands have made their names in the Indian textile industry of India. The small business owners have bootstrapped their startups and have made a turnover to a touch of crores. The ease of sending the parcels within and outside the country has also a big contribution in boosting the sales of any online Brand. Digital payments through Net Banking, Paytm, and UPI also ease the process of buying for any client. The cultural diversity of India, various festivals, weddings, and different seasons motivate the buying of apparel and Home linens among people of India and Indians living in a foreign land. To feel connected to their roots and enjoy the festivals Indians staying abroad also opt for online shopping through Instagram and this boosts the sales of a budding entrepreneur and also favors the Start-up India program of our country.

The digital transformation, people's urge to look good, the increase in disposable incomes of households, and working women and their choices to buy have also given a push to these small business owners. Not only apparel or Home linens but many other brands which make products of crochet, Macramé, Jute, Bamboo, and Clay have made their names in the market through Digital marketing and have reached across the globe with the help of wonderful logistics with tracking facility these days from the comfort of any iPhone and Android-based application.

References

1. http://thebetterindia.com
2. www.bluehost.com
3. https://yourstory.com/herstory/2023/01/mother-daughter-chikankari-venture-shark-tank-india
4. www.fabriclore.com
5. http://theindianethnicco.com

11.

A QUALITATIVE ANALYSIS ON THE DIFFERENT AREAS OF SKILL DEVELOPMENT IN COMMUNITY SCIENCE

Dr. Lakshmi. S

Assistant Professor, BNVCTE

Thiruvallam, Thiruvananthapuram

Kerala

Email: lakshmibinu79@gmail.com

Abstract

Community science, also known as citizen science or participatory science, refers to the involvement of community members in scientific research, data collection, analysis, and decision-making processes. It is a collaborative approach that bridges the gap between professional scientists and the general public, allowing non-experts to contribute to scientific endeavours. Community science promotes inclusivity, democratizes scientific research, and harnesses the collective power of communities to address local challenges, contribute to scientific knowledge, and drive positive change. Skills play a crucial role in community science by empowering individuals and communities to engage in scientific inquiry, data collection, analysis, and problem-solving. Here are some key reasons why skills are important in community science. Skills in community science enhance scientific literacy, promote collaboration, foster innovation, address local challenges, uphold ethical standards, and empower individuals and communities to become active contributors in scientific research and problem-solving. Developing skills in community science is an ongoing process. It requires a combination of theoretical knowledge, practical experience, and active engagement with communities and scientists. By continuously learning and contributing to community science projects, we can make meaningful contributions to scientific research and community well-being.

Keywords: Skill development, Strategies, Participation

1. Introduction

Community science can take many forms, depending on the nature of the research and the needs of the community. Some common examples include:

1.1. Environmental monitoring

Community members collect data on air quality, water quality, biodiversity, or other environmental indicators to track changes and identify potential issues or threats.

1.2. Public health initiatives

Communities engage in data collection and monitoring to identify and address health concerns, such as tracking disease outbreaks or monitoring pollution levels.

1.3. Astronomical observations

Amateur astronomers contribute to scientific research by observing celestial objects, monitoring changes, and sharing their observations with professional scientists.

1.4. Wildlife conservation

Community members participate in monitoring programs to track animal populations, migration patterns, or habitat changes, contributing to conservation efforts.

Developing skills in community science involves a combination of learning and practical experience. It requires the equal involvement of both theoretical and practical knowledge. Certain strategies that can be widely used for the skill development programs in community science are detailed below:

Education and training

Start by acquiring a solid foundation of scientific knowledge and research methods through formal education. Pursue relevant courses or programs in fields such as environmental science, biology, ecology, or citizen science. These educational opportunities can provide you with a theoretical understanding of scientific principles and methodologies.

Participate in citizen science projects

Engage in citizen science initiatives that involve collaborative research between scientists and the public. These projects often focus on data collection, analysis, and interpretation. By participating, you can learn about scientific protocols, data gathering techniques, and analytical tools.

Join local science organizations

Get involved with local science organizations, such as naturalist societies, environmental groups, or community science networks. These organizations often host workshops, training sessions, and events related to community science. By participating, you can learn from experienced individuals, share knowledge, and collaborate on scientific projects.

Attend workshops and conferences

Look out for workshops and conferences focused on community science. These events bring together researchers, practitioners, and enthusiasts to share knowledge, present research findings, and discuss best practices. Attending such events can expose you to cutting-edge research, emerging methodologies, and networking opportunities.

Online courses and resources

Take advantage of online courses and resources dedicated to community science. Platforms like Coursera, edX, or even YouTube offer courses or tutorials on scientific methodologies, data analysis, and citizen science projects. These resources allow you to learn at your own pace and explore specific areas of interest.

Volunteer with scientists

Seek opportunities to volunteer with scientists or research institutions involved in community science projects. By working closely with professionals, you can gain hands-on experience in data collection, research methodologies, and scientific analysis. This experiential learning can greatly enhance your skills and understanding of community science.

Collaborate with local communities

Engage with local communities and work together to address scientific questions or environmental challenges. By collaborating with community members, one can learn about their perspectives, traditional knowledge, and the specific issues they face. This approach fosters mutual learning and empowers communities to actively participate in scientific research.

Practice data analysis and interpretation

Familiarizing oneself with data analysis techniques, statistical tools, and data visualization methods commonly used in community science will help in developing skills in interpreting and communicating scientific findings in a way that is accessible to a broader audience.

Developing skills in community science is an ongoing process. It requires a combination of theoretical knowledge, practical experience, and active engagement with communities and scientists. By continuously learning and contributing to community science projects, we can make meaningful contributions to scientific research and community well-being.

2. Categories of skills required in community science

2.1. Data collection skills

Learn how to collect accurate and reliable data by understanding various data collection methods, such as field observations, surveys, specimen collection, or water quality testing. Develop skills in following scientific protocols, recording data effectively, and ensuring data quality.

2.2. Research design and methodology

Gain proficiency in designing research projects, formulating research questions, and selecting appropriate methodologies. Learn about sampling techniques, experimental design, and data management strategies specific to community science projects.

2.3. Data analysis and interpretation

Acquire skills in analyzing and interpreting data collected through community science projects. This includes learning statistical analysis techniques, using software tools like R or Python, and applying appropriate visualization methods to communicate findings effectively.

2.4. Collaboration and communication

Develop skills in collaboration and effective communication to work with diverse stakeholders, including scientists, community members, and policymakers. Practice active listening, effective facilitation, and the ability to convey scientific information in accessible language.

2.5. Community Engagement and Empowerment

Learn strategies for engaging and empowering local communities in scientific research. Develop skills in building relationships, fostering trust, and involving community members in all stages of the research process, from project design to implementation and dissemination of results.

3. Strategies for developing skill development in community Science

3.1. Environmental monitoring and assessment

Gain expertise in monitoring and assessing environmental indicators such as air quality, water quality, biodiversity, or climate variables. Learn about appropriate monitoring techniques, data interpretation, and reporting to contribute to environmental stewardship and decision-making.

3.2. Science communication and public outreach

Enhance your skills in science communication to effectively communicate scientific concepts and findings to diverse audiences. This includes writing for non-scientific audiences, public speaking, creating engaging visuals, and utilizing social media platforms to disseminate information.

3.3. Ethical considerations

Understand the ethical considerations and responsibilities associated with community science. Develop skills in ensuring informed consent, maintaining confidentiality, and addressing potential conflicts of interest. Stay updated on ethical guidelines and practices in scientific research involving communities.

4. Qualities or abilities needed for skill development in community science

4.1. Curiosity and open-mindedness

A curious and open-minded approach is essential in community science. Being curious encourages exploration, asking questions, and seeking new knowledge. Open-mindedness allows for embracing diverse perspectives, ideas, and solutions, fostering collaboration with community members.

4.2. Empathy and cultural competence

Developing empathy and cultural competence is crucial for working with diverse communities. Understanding and appreciating different cultural contexts, beliefs, and values helps establish meaningful connections and respectful relationships with community members.

4.3. Communication Skills

Effective communication is vital for community science. Strong verbal and written communication skills enable clear and concise exchange of ideas, active listening, and the ability to convey scientific concepts to both scientific and non-scientific audiences.

4.4. Collaboration and teamwork

Community science often involves collaborating with various stakeholders, including community members, scientists, and policymakers. Building effective collaborative relationships, practicing teamwork, and valuing diverse perspectives contribute to successful community science initiatives.

4.5. Adaptability and flexibility

Community science projects can be dynamic and unpredictable. Being adaptable and flexible allows for adjusting plans, methodologies, and approaches based on changing circumstances or community needs. This quality helps navigate challenges and find creative solutions.

4.6. Problem-solving skills

Developing strong problem-solving skills is valuable in community science. Being able to identify research gaps, design appropriate methodologies, analyze data, and find practical solutions to challenges encountered during the research process enhances the effectiveness of community science projects.

4.7. Ethical awareness and integrity

Ethical considerations are critical in community science. Having a strong sense of ethical awareness, integrity, and a commitment to conducting research in a responsible and respectful manner ensures the well-being of communities and the appropriate use of data collected.

4.8. Resilience and perseverance

Community science projects may face obstacles, setbacks, or complex issues. Developing resilience and perseverance helps overcome challenges, learn from failures, and stay motivated to achieve project goals despite difficulties.

4.9. Data literacy and analytical thinking

Strong data literacy skills, including the ability to analyze and interpret scientific data, are essential for community science. Developing analytical thinking skills supports effective data analysis, identification of patterns or trends, and drawing meaningful conclusions.

4.10. Reflective practice

Engaging in reflective practice fosters continuous learning and improvement in community science. Reflecting on experiences, evaluating methodologies, and seeking feedback help refine skills, address biases, and enhance the overall quality of community science projects.

References

1. Diepan, V.A. (2000). *Households and their spatial-energetic practices. Searching for sustainable urban forms*. (Doctoral dissertation, Faculty of Spatial Sciences, University of Groningen, Netherlands).
2. Schwartz, S.H., & Howard, J.A. (1981). A normative decision- making model of altruism. In J.P. Rushtan (Ed). Altruism and helping behaviour. *Social, Personality and Developmental Perspectives,8,* 189-211.
3. Ajzen, I. (1991). The theory of planned behavior. *Organizational Behavior and Human decision processes, 50,* 179-211.

12.

MILLETS: SUSTAINABLE WAY TO FOOD AND NUTRITIONAL SECURITY

Dr Preeti Verma[1], Naresh Kumar Agarwal[2], Anita Raj[3]

[1]Subject Matter Specialist (Home Science), [2]Subject Matter Specialist (Horticulture), [3](Lecturer)

[1,2]Krishi Vigyan Kendra, Banasthali Vidyapith, [3]Govt. PG. College, Panchkula, Chandigarh

Email: preetiv335@gmail.com

Abstract

Today increasing population is the main concern in food and nutritional security. Malnutrition including both over nutrition and under nutrition are serious concern in todys's era. There is a need to add such types of food which solve above mentioned problems. Being a highly nutritious and low input crop, millet fits perfectly to solve the nutrition related problems. In millets, Sorghum, Pearl millet, Finger millet, Kodo millet, Little millet, Foxtail millet, Proso millet and Barnyard millet are included. They are a good source of energy, carbohydrates, protein, fat, mineral and vitamin rendering good human health. Consumption of these millets help to reduce malnutrition as well as life style related diseases *vis;* obesity, diabetes and cardiovascular diseases.

Millet is the perfect food for people suffering from celiac disease hence inclusion of these precious millet in our diet is an economical way to achieve nutritional security as they do not require much needed resources to grow and highly resistant to any diseases and pest. So the present review article focuses on nutritive value of millets, their health benefits and processing techniques for their enhanced consumption.

1. Introduction

Millet is a term used to a small seeded annual grasses belong to Poaceae family. They are generally grown in semi arid areas and are staple food in that particular area. Millets are cultivated in past 50 years for human consumption and fodder purpose. Millets are cultivated in China, Greece, Africa, Egypt and India. In India, major millet producing states are Karnatka, Tamil Nadu, Kerla, Andhra Pradesh, Telangana, Hyderabad, Jharkhand, Uttarakhand and Madya Pradesh. Millets are classified as major and minor millet. Sorghum, Pearl millet and Finger millet come under the category of major millet while in minor millets, Kodo millet, Little millet, Foxtail millet, Proso millet and Barnyard millet are included. Millets are low input crops. They can tolerate drought and adverse climatic conditions. Considering it a super food, it is also known as **Shri Anna**. Millets are a good source of macro as well as micro nutrients. Besides their nutritional values, they possess neutraceutical properties. They are gluten free and acid free forming food. Consumption of millet helps to reduce the risk of anaemia, malnutrition, obesity, diabetes, cardiovascular diseases, Celiac diseases and much more. Though cereals (wheat and rice) are major crop of our country and provide food security but when they are compared with millets, millets are superior to cereals in terms of their nutritional and phytochemical profile (Kimeera & Sucharitha, 2019). Consumption of millet is limited to the area where it is grown. Hence there is a need to prepare value added products of millet for increasing its consumption beyond the particular area with improved shelf life and availability throughout the year. This review article focuses on the millet nutritive value, health benefits and their value added products.

2. Sorghum

Sorghum millet or Jwar (*Sorghum bicolor*) is an erect, tall and annual grass with 1-2 meter plant height. It has long leaves and clusters of grains are found on the top of its stems. The size of grain is small and round with hard outer covering. In India, Sorghum is cultivated in Andhra Pradesh, Bihar, Chhattisgarh, Gujrat, Haryana, Jharkhand, Karnataka, Madhya Pradesh, Maharashtra, Nagaland, Odisa, Rajasthan, Tamil Nadu, Telangana and Uttar Pradesh. Sorghum is a good source of nutrients especially energy, protein, fibre, vitamin and minerals. In vitamin, it is rich in Beta-carotene, thiamine, riboflavin, folic acid and in minerals; it is an abundant source of iron, calcium, sodium and potassium. Sorghum also has a wax policosanol which plays an important role in reducing cholesterol level in human body. Consumption of sorghum is a safe food for the people suffering from malnutrition, anaemia, obesity, cardiovascular diseases and celiac disease (Liu et al., 2012).

Value added products of sorghum increases its availability in our diet. The preparation method of recipe of sorghum known as **Sorghum Burelu** is given below.

2.1. Sorghum Burelu

Ingredients: Sorghum flour-200 gm, Wheat flour-100 gm, Jaggery-100 gm, Cardamom-2 gm, Fennel seed-30 gm, Ghee for frying.

Preparation method: Except Ghee, mix all the ingredients together. Add one teaspoon ghee in it and make a dough. Make it into a round balls and deep fry it (Rao et al., 2021).

3. Pearl millet

Pearl millet or Bajra (*Pennisetum glaucum*) is a upright bunch grass with tillers from the base and has an extensive root system. It is a leafy plant with leaf blades that are 1-2 meter tall. In India, Pearl millet is cultivated in Rajasthan, Andhra Pradesh, Bihar, Gujrat, Haryana, Himachal Pradesh, Jammu, Kashmir, Jharkhand, Karnataka, Madhya Pradesh, Maharashtra, Odisha, Punjab, Tamil Nadu, Telangana and Uttar Pradesh. Pearl millet is a good source of macro and micro nutrients. It has highest amont of iron among all millets making it most suitable millet to prevent and cure iron deficiency anaemia in a cost effective manner (Shobana et al., 2013).

Value added products of Pearl millet increases its availability in our diet. The preparation method of recipe of Pearl millet known as **Pearl millet rusk** is given below.

3.1. Pearl millet rusk

Ingredients: Pearl millet flour-200 gm, Butter-100 gm, Baking powder-5 gm, Egg-3, Castor sugar-50 gm, Vanilla essence-1tsp, Baking soda-1 gm.

Preparation method: Add butter and castor sugar and beat it with hand beater. Add eggs one by one to this mixture until it becomes fluffiness. Add pearl millet flour, baking powder and vanilla essence mix thoroughly. Simultaneously pre heat the oven at 180^{0c} for 15 minutes. Pour the above batter on a greased cake pan and bake at 180^{oc} for 20 minutes. After cooling cut into square pieces and bake it in an oven at 180 oc for 20 minutes till it gets crisp in nature (Rao et al., 2021).

4. Finger millet

Finger millet or Ragi (*Eleusine coracana*) owning to the appearance of the head of the grain comprising five spikes and thus resembling the five fingers attached to the palm of hand. Finger millet crop has 5-8 tillers with 0.75 to 0.8 meter height. In India, Finger millet is cultivated in Andhra Pradesh, Bihar, Chhatisgarh, Gujarat, Himachal Pradesh, Jammu and Kashmir, Jharkhand, Karnataka, Madhya Pradesh, Maharashtra, Oddisa, Sikkim, Tamil Nadu, Telangana, Uttarakhand and West Bengal. Finger millet is a good source of protein especially methionine amino acid, calcium, iron and fibre. In all millets, it has highest amount of calcium making it a good food for bone and teeth health (Verma & Patel, 2012). Finger millets are used to make products like Ragi cake, Ragi Puddings and Ragi Porridge. In Nepal, Finger Millet is used to make bear.

Value added products of finger millet increases its availability in our diet. The preparation method of recipe of finger millet known as **Finger millet peanut Chikki** is given below.

4.1. Finger millet peanut chikki

<u>Ingredients:</u> Finger millet flour-80 gm, Peanut-100 gm, Jaggery-100 gm, Ghee-20 gm

<u>Preparation method:</u> Roast and coarsely crush the peanuts in grinder. Heat jaggery with 1 tbsp water until it gives thick consistency. Boil the syrup until it shows hard crack consistency. Add finger millet flour, peanut, ghee to the syrup and mix it thoroughly. Grease a tray with a lttle amount of ghee and speard the mixture. Roll it flat using a rolling pin. After cooling, cut into square shape (Rao et al., 2021).

5. Porso millet

Proso millet or Cheena (*Panicum miliaceum*) is also called as common millet, Broom corn and white millet. Proso millet is erect annual millet with 1.2-1.5 meter plant length and free tillering and tufted with a shallow root system. It's stem is cylindrical with simple alternate and hairy leaves. In India, Proso millet is cultivated in Himachal Pradesh. Proso millet is a good source of micro and macro nutrients especially in niacin which plays an important role in preventing 3 D diseases that includes Diarrhoea, Dementia and Dermatitis (Rathore et al., 2016).

The preparation method of recipe of Proso millet known as **Proso millet Cheese ball** is given below.

5.1. Proso millet cheese ball

<u>Ingredients:</u> Proso millet flour-100 gm, Wheat flour-10 gm, Potato-6 gm, Carrot-6 gm, Chilli powder-2 gm, Ginger paste-5 gm, Corn flour-80 gm, salt-3 gram, Cheese-40 gm, Bread powder-20 gm, Vegetable oil for frying.

Preparation method: Boil carrot, potatoes in cooker and cook for 4-5 whistes and mash it in a bowl. Add finely chopped green chillies, salt, ginger garlic paste, corn flour maida and proso millet flour and mix well. Make square cheese pieces. Take mashed potato, carrot and above proso millet mixture, make small balls and flatten balls with cheese pieces. Make it into round balls. Mix corn flour in water and keep it aside. Dip these balls in corn flour water batter and roll in bread crumbs. Keep all these cheese balls in fridge for 20 minutes. Deep fry until they becomes golden brown colour. Serve hot with tomato or chilli sauce (Rao et al., 2021).

6. Kodo millet

Kodo millet (*Paspalum scrobiculatum*) plant is an erect annual with hairy nodes and fully sheated solid internodes. It is a monocot and grows with the height of four feet. Kodo millet is cultivated in Andra Pradesh, Gujarat, Himachal Pradesh, Madhya Pradesh, Tamil Nadu and Uttar Pradesh. Kodo millet comes under the category of minor millet and has good amount of antioxidant, phytochemicals and fibre(Sarita & Singh, 2016). Kodo millet resembles rice. It is easily digestible. Kodo millet plays an important role in curing and treating joint pain and knee pain.

The preparation method of recipe of Kodo millet known as **Kodo millet Poha Tikki** is given below.

6.1. Kodo millet poha tikki

Ingredients: Kodo Millet-100 gm, Corn flour-20 gm, Wheat bread crumbs-40 gm, Red chilli powder-2 gm, Turmeric powder-3 gm, Ajwain-2 gm, Garam masala-2 gm, Amchur powder-2 gm and salt to taste.

Preparation method: Wash Kodo millet flakes in water and then squeeze out the excess water using a muslin cloth. Mix all the mentioned ingredients with the above flakes to get a mixture. Make lemon shape balls out of the mixture. Slighly flatten the mixture balls with your palm to make a kodo millet poha Tikki. Dip the kodo millet poha Tikki in corn flour slurry and roll them in bread crumbs. Heat oil in a pan and fry the Tikki and cook on both sides till it becomes crispy. Serve along with some tomato sauce or mint chutney (Rao et al., 2021).

7. Foxtail millet

Foxtail millet or Kangani (*Eleusine coracana*)is also called German millet and Italian millet. Foxtail millet is an erect annual grass, fast growing, leafy and tufted with 0.9-2 meter plant height. It has a dense root system and tillers from the base. Foxtail millet is cultivated inAndhra Pradesh, Gujarat, Karnatak, Sikkim, Tamil Nadu, Telangana and Tripura. Foxtail millet plays an important role in curing and preventing diabetes by maintaining blood glucose level. It also maintains heart health due to its magnesium content (Radhika et al., 2019).The preparation method of recipe of Foxtail Millet known as **Foxtail Millet Chocolate Ice Cream** is given below.

7.1. Foxtail Millet Chocolate Ice Cream

Ingredients: Foxtail millet rice-100 gm, Whip cream-200 gm, Cocoa powder-20 gm. Condensed milk-100 gm and Choco chips- 5gm.

Preparation method: Soak the foxtail millet rice in excess amount of water for overnight. Wash the grains properly and grind the millets by adding water in a 1:1 ratio. Extract the milk from the foxtail millet and filter it. Put the whipped cream in a blender and mix it till it becomes silky and fluffy. add cocoa powder and condensed milk to the above mix and blend it again in the mixer. Add foxtail milk to the above mixture and blend till it becomes fluffy. Transfer it to a bowl and keep in the freezer for 8 hours. Now foxtail chocolate ice cream is ready to serve as a delicious frozen dessert (Rao et al., 2021).

8. Little millet

Little millet or Kutki (*Panicum sumatrense*) is cultivated in Arunachal Pradesh, Assam, Bihar, Chhatisgarh, Jammu-Kahsmir, Maharashtra, Nagaland, Oddisha, Rajasthan and Tamil Nadu. Little millet is called little but not less than its nutritional value Little millet has a good amount of vitamin and mineral. It also has essential fatty acid. It is also ideal ingredient for making kheer instead of rice. Because of its high fibre content, it is suitable for obese person (Bruntha et al., 2014).The preparation method of recipe of Little Millet known as **Little Millet Tea** is given below.

8.1. Little Millet tea

Ingredients: Dehulled Little Millet- 50 gm, Sugar -5 gm, Tea powder -1 tsp, Pepper -1 gm, Cardamum- 2 pods, Clove -1, Dry ginger powder- 2 gm, Nutmeg powder -1 gm and Water as required.

Preparation method: Soak dehulled little millet for 2 hour and wash it properly. Now grind the grain by using required amount of water and filter for 50 ml of little millet milk. Boil all the spices with tea powder and 1 cup of water in a vessel under medium flave for 10 minutes. Add sugar and little millet milk to above spice water. Filter and serve it hot (Rao et al., 2021).

9. Barnyard millet

Barnyard millet or Sawa *(Echinochloa esculenta)* is the fourth most produced minor millet. Barnyard millet is cultivated in Sikkim, Uttar Pradesh and Uttarakhand. Barnyard millet has a good amount of protein and dietary fibre including both soluble and insoluble portion. Because of high fibre content, its consumption is useful in diabetes most effective in reducing blood glucose, lipid levels and obesity. Barnyard millet is also useful for the person having sedentary life style. Barnyard also has essential fatty acids linoleic acid, palmitic and oleic acid which are essential for maintaining skin health (Gull et al., 2014). Barnyard millet is also. The preparation method of recipe of Barnyard millet known as **Barnyard millet Carrot Truffles** is given below.

9.1. Barnyard millet carrot truffles

<u>Ingredients:</u> Barnyard millet flour-50 gm, Sugar- 60 gm, Carrot- 100 gm, Almond- 10 gm, Cardamom Powder-1 gm, Coconut Powder- 50 gm and water as required.

<u>Preparation method:</u> Add grated carrot to the pan and saute them until raw flavour goes off. Add sugar, close the lid and cook until it melts. Open the lid, add barnyard flour, coconut powder and cardamom powder and mix well. Take some portion of the prepared mixture and roll to make small lemon size balls. Coat or roll the above barnyard millet carrot truffles into desiccated coconut powder. Serve as a healthy millet snack (Rao et al., 2021).

Nutrient content of millets per 100 gram

Millet	Energy (Kcal)	Carbohydrate (gram)	Protein (gram)	Fat (gram)	Mineral (gram)	Fibre (gram)	Iron (miligram)	Calcium (miligram)
Sorghum	329	70.7	10.4	3.1	1.2	2.0	5.4	25
Pearl	363	67	11.8	4.8	2.2	2.2	11	42
Finger	336	72	7.3	1.3	2.7	3.6	3.9	344
Kodo	353	65.9	8.3	1.4	2.6	5.2	1.7	35
Little	329	67	7.7	4.7	1.7	7.6	9.3	17
Foxtail	351	60.2	12.3	4.3	4	6.7	2.8	31
Proso	354	70.4	12.5	1.1	1.9	5.2	2.9	8.0
Barnyard	300	65.5	6.2	4.8	3.7	13.6	18.6	22

10. Health benefits of millets

In present scenario people are very conscious about health. Millet is hidden source for health promoting phytochemicals, and antioxidant as nutraceuticals as well as functional food.

10.1. Good for diabetic person

Millets are useful for the patients suffering from diabetes mellitus because of having complex carbohydrate. Millet improve the functioning of enzyme aldose reductase which plays an important role in preventing accumulation of sorbitol and decrease the risk of diabetes. Millets are also important in delay wound healing process. Studies on millet consumption showed the lower risk of diabetes mellitus as compared to cereal based diets. Results showed that people who consumed millets in diet, found to have low level of glucose (Alajaji & El-Adawy, 2006).

10.2. Cancer curing

Millets are rich sources of antioxidants (Phenolic acid, tannin, and phytate) which are helpful in scavenging free radicals produced during oxidation-reduction process in our body reducing the risk of cancer. Lenolic acid found in millets has tumor preventing properties. Sorghum has good amount of tannins and polyphenols showing anticarcinogenic and antimutagenic property. A recent study has showed that millets found to be effective in the prevention of cancer initiation and progression in vitro (Adebiyi et al., 2018).

10.3. Good for celiac disease

Millets are the best option for the patients suffering from Celiac disease. In Celiac disease, a person is not able to digest wheat as it has gluten protein. Millets don't have gluten making it the most suitable food in such type of disease and help to reduce bowel irritation caused by wheat consumption (Kameera & Sucharitha, 2019).

10.4. Cardiovascular health

Millets are a good source of calcium, potassium and magnesium which in turn play an important role in cardiovascular health. Cholesterol-lowering property of Millets is because of its phyto chemicals properties. Hence, consumption of millets reduce cholesterol and the chances of hypertension which in turn reduces the chances of atherosclerosis and cardiac arrest (Rani et al., 2018).

11. Conclusions

In conclusion, millets are nutrient dense traditional grains that have a variety of health benefits. Icing on the cake is that they are low input crop, resistant to climate change, drought resistant and insect-pest resistant making it a super food for poor community. Consumption of millet reduces malnutrition and anaemia and a number of diseases. By value addition of these millets, their consumption can be increased providing nutritional security to the Nation.

References

1. Alajaji, S.A.,& El-Adawy, T.A. (2006). Nutritional composition of chickpea (*Cicer arietinum L.*) as affected by microwave cooking and other traditional cooking methods. Journal of Food Composition and Analysis, 19(8):806–812.
2. Adebiyi, J., Obadina, A., Adebo, O., & Kayitesi, E. (2018). Fermented and malted millet products in Africa: Expedition from traditional/ethnic foods to industrial value added products. Critical reviews in Food Science and nutrition, 58(3):463–474.
3. Gull, A., Jan, R., Nayik, G. A., Prasad, K., & Kumar, P. (2014). Significance of finger millet in nutrition,

health and value added products: a review. Journal of Environmental Science, Computer Science and Engineering and Technology, 3(3), 1601-1608.

4. Issoufou, A., Elhadji, G., Mahamadou., &Le G. (2013).Millets: Nutritional composition, some health benefits and processing-A Review. *Emirates Journal of Food and Agriculture* 25(7):501-508.
5. Kimeera, A., & Sucharitha, K.V. (2019).Millets-Review on Nutritional Profiles and Health Benefits. *International Journal of Recent Scientific Research*, 07(I):33943-33948.
6. Liu, J., Tang, X., Zhang, Y.,& Zhao, W. (2012). Determination of the volatile composition in brown millet, milled millet and millet bran by gas chromatography/mass spectrometry. *Molecules*, 17:2271–82.
7. Bruntha,P., Vijayabharathi,R., Sathyabama,S.,Malleshi,N.G., &Priyadarisini, V.B.(2014), Health benefits of finger millet (Eleusine coracana L.) polyphenols and dietary fiber: a review.*Journal of Food Science and Technology*, 51(6):1021-1040.
8. Radhika, V.A., Kaur, M., Thakur, P., Chauhan, D., Rizvi, Q. U., Jan, S.,& Kumar, K. (2019). Development and Nutritional Evaluation of Multigrain Gluten free cookies and pasta products. *Current Research in Nutrition and Food Science*, 3(7):842-843.
9. Rani., S, Singh, R., Sehrawat, R., Kaur, B.P., & Upadhyay, A (2018). Pearl millet processing: a review, Nutrition & Food Science, 48 (1):30-44.

10. Sarita.,& Singh, E. (2016). Potential of Millets: Nutrients Composition and Health Benefits. *Journal of Scientific and Innovative Research*, 5(2):46-50.
11. Shobana, S., Krishnaswami, K., Sudha, V., Malleshi, N.G., Anjana R.M., Palaniappan, L.,& Mohan, V. (2013). Finger Millet (Ragi, Eleusine coracana L.): A Review Of Its Nutritional Properties, Processing, and Plausible Health Benifits. *Advance in Food and Nutrition Research*, 69:1-3.
12. Rathore,S., Singh, K.,&KumarV. (2016). Millet Grain Processing, Utilization and Its Role in Health Promotion:A Review. International Journal of Nutrition and Food Sciences, 5(5): 318-329.
13. Rao, B.D., Srinu, M., Lakshmi, K.V., Kiranmai, E.,& Tonapi, V.A. (2021). Millet Recipes-A Healthy Choice. Indian Institute of Millet Research, Hyderabad, 81:11-186.
14. Verma, V.,& Patel, S. (2012), Nutritional security and value added products from finger millets (Ragi).*Journal of Applicable Chemistry*, 1(4):485-489.

LIST OF PUBLISHED BOOKS

1. Gupta K and Jain M. Vridhopayogi Vyanjan: Vridhjano ke liye Upcharatmak Pak Vidhiyan. Abhinav Prakashan. Ajmer. 2016. ISBN: 978-938418946-4

This book contains more than 65 healthy food recipes developed, prepared and clinically verified by myself alone, tailored with the nutritional needs of the geriatric population.

2. Gupta K. Community Science and Sustainable Community Development. Lambart Academic Publication. Germany 2021. ISBN: 978-620419757-9

This book provides excellent research data related to different aspects of community which will be helpful to strengthen the sustainability of a community in terms of health, nutrition, wellness and economy.

3. Gupta K. 75 years of Indian Independence: Food and Nutritional Achievements, Opportunities and Challenges (Volume 1). Notion Press. Chennai. 2022. ISBN: 979-888883053-6

4. Gupta K. 75 years of Indian Independence: Food and Nutritional Achievements, Opportunities and Challenges (Volume 2). Notion Press. Chennai. 2022. ISBN: 979-888883757-3

5. Gupta K. 75 years of Indian Independence: Food and Nutritional Achievements, Opportunities and Challenges (Volume 3). Notion Press. Chennai. 2022. ISBN: 979-888909005-2

These three books provide enriched research data pertaining to various aspects of health, lifestyle, tourism, agriculture, antenatal or post natal diet, nutritional status, cognition and nutrition, etc., that will be extremely helpful to improve quality of life of the individuals ultimately making healthy and sustainable community.

6. Gupta K. Aazadi ka Amrit Mahotsav: Community Science Achievements, Opportunities and Challenges. BlueRose One Publishers. India. 2023. ISBN: 978-935704938-2

This book is particularly based on different disciplines of community science, i.e., food science and nutrition, food security, advancement in food preservation and processing, sustainable breeding and cultivation approaches in agriculture, importance of prebiotics, role of therapeutic diet, importance of nutrition for pregnant ladies and children, how cognitive development is affected by nutritional status of the children, spiritual development, skill based learning system DEASA, effect of social media on community development.

7. Gupta K. Nutrition Education: An Important Pillar of Health. Notion Press. Chennai. 2023. ISBN: 979-888959915-9

This book is particularly based on different topics of nutrition science, i.e., importance of nutrition in daily life, flavours of Bengal, flavours of Ramadan, Indian spices, celebrate a world of flavours, nutrition in bed bound patients, why nutrition is essential and importance of homemade pickles in daily diet.

8. Gupta K, Bhushan V, Pandey A. Issues with Girls. Notion Press. Chennai. 2023. ISBN: 979-889026221-9

This book is particularly based on different topics related to girls and women, i.e., change in education to bring empowerment, mental hygiene, health and diet management, rise in health problems: A wake up call, girls hygiene and nutrients, letting the girls grow naturally, nutrition for girls, optimal nutrition, good health and wellbeing,: are we there yet?, women's leadership and role model for girls, empowering girls: dare to dream, baby girl: beautiful miracles.

9. Gupta K, Tripathi KM, Meena N, Sukhwal I, Soni V. Recent Trends in Community Science. BlueRose One Publishers. India. 2023. ISBN: 978-935819026-7

This book is based on different area of community science, i.e., parenting techniques and changes in parenting over the time, association between eating out and childhood obesity, rural participation and community development, ergonomics for everyone, kitchen ergonomics, use of unconventional fibres in textile industry, sustainable techniques for dye application (textile industry), spiritual development, therapeutic nutrition, impact of dietary habits on people suffering from polycystic ovarian syndrome (PCOS), millets: heritage of India, *terminalia arjuna* herb and its impact on hypercholesterolemia's patients, black cumin seeds, development disorders of children and homoeopathic treatment, success stories of women entrepreneurs from fields of community science.

10. Gupta K, Katiyar P, Meena S, Tripathi KM,. Millets: The Miracle of Nature. Notion Press. Chennai. 2023. ISBN: 979-889066606-2

This book is particularly based on topics such as millets- the nutria-cereal, magical grains, millets- the climate resilient nutria cereals, India's treasury: millets as dietary accessory, therapeutic role of millets in daily life, nutritional impact of millets on pregnant mothers, economic aspects of millets etc,.

11. Gupta K, Cherian B, Ramalakshmi, Harjai K. Health and Wellness (A basic guide to obtain good health). Notion Press. Chennai. 2023. ISBN: 979-889067222-3

Chapters of this book entitled "Health and Wellness (A basic guide to obtain good health)" particularly based on topics such as Blood, breathing & thoughts, Meditation, yoga, silence and prayer, Mind-body connection: Using yoga to enhance maternal health, Improve your low self-esteem with blessings of yoga and meditation, Food habits, Nutrition for health, Biogreens: the immunity booster, Role of nutrition in obesity, No health without mental health, Ayurveda for holistic health care, Homoeopathic biochemic treatment, Palliative care, Functional foods in cardiovascular disease, Union government initiatives to provide affordable, accessible, and quality healthcare for all.

12. Gupta K, Gaur V, Kumari R, Mishra S, Arya L, Mukharjee G. Health for All. Notion Press. Chennai. 2023. ISBN: 979-889133024-5

The edited book volume is primarily intended to be a collection of peer reviewed and plagiarism free chapters written by research scholars, academicians, scientists, doctors and faculty members of their respective fields. Chapters of this book entitled “Health for All” particularly based on topics such as sustainable innovation strategies in public health, application of technology in healthcare, world health organization’s policies on world nutrition, the invisible threat of food borne diseases, obesity in affluent societies and its effect, role of nutrition education, treatment of diseases using different medical systems, non communicable diseases through workplace wellness initiatives, immunization program and serum banking in India.

www.ingramcontent.com/pod-product-compliance
Lightning Source LLC
LaVergne TN
LVHW021147160826
845679LV00024B/2080

* 9 7 9 8 8 9 1 8 6 0 8 7 2 *